THE POCKET
HOMEBREW
HANDBOOK

THE POCKET HOMEBREW HANDBOOK

75 recipes for the aspiring backyard brewer

Dave Law and
Beshlie Grimes

DOG 'n' BONE

First edition published in 2012 by CICO Books
This paperback edition published in 2015
by Dog 'n' Bone Books
an imprint of Ryland Peters & Small Ltd
20–21 Jockey's Fields   341 E 116th St
London WC1R 4BW   New York, NY 10029

www.rylandpeters.com

10 9 8 7 6 5 4 3 2 1

A CIP catalog record for this book is available from the Library of
Congress and the British Library.

ISBN-13: 978 1 909313 61 3

Printed in China

Editor: Caroline West
Design concept: Ashley Western
Design for reformat: Jerry Goldie
Photographer: Gavin Kingcome
Stylist: Luis Peral-Aranda

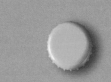

Contents

From Monk to Punk

If you have picked up this book, it is because you have a passion for beer big enough to make you want to brew it. I started brewing beer while at art school if only for two simple reasons—to have cheap beer to sell to mates and to get sloshed. Yes, it is an unfashionable thing to say these days but, let's be honest, we're all adults.

I like to think I have grown up since then (although my wife is probably the best judge of that). A beer for me now is more about taste, but it still helps me to relax and I still like the sensation of having one or two more than I should. There are dozens of great books on the subject of homebrewing, so what is it that makes this book different? Well, I'm going to try and cut through the mystique, the waffle, and the scientific attention to detail. Some books, for example, encourage wrapping duvets around wort buckets or hanging grain sacks along broomsticks. While the advice (and knowledge it is based on) is genuine, I hope to get you brewing with as simple and efficient an explanation and method as possible. After all, from the Sumerians through to the Victorians, beer production was little more than happy coincidence until Louis Pasteur (1822–1895) rocked up with his treatise on how to control those pesky yeasts. Until then everyone knew how to do it, but not why or how it really worked. The main events that need to occur are quite simple:

- The conversion of starches and carbohydrates to sugars

- The subsequent conversion of sugars to alcohol

- The addition of hops and adjuncts to add flavor and to preserve

Like many things, you can get as involved in the detail as you want, but it's not needed to begin with. Follow the simple steps, tips, and guidelines outlined in this book and you will be brewing your own in no time.

Today, you don't need to know all the complicated equations and go back to your school books to revisit algebra. You can pick up hop-rate apps and brewing programs on the Internet that will do all that for you. Your local brew-shop staff will usually be enthusiasts, too, and there are many fora to check out for help should you need it.

If I were to point out the single most likely factor that can wipe out your chances of brewing a decent beer—and jeopardizing your beery success—it would be dirt. Any muck in your equipment will undermine the chances of your homebrewed beer giving you a wide grin of satisfaction. So sanitize, sanitize, and sanitize again. And, please, don't just clean with your eyes—you will be amazed how many people do, much to their detriment.

Just For Fun: Words For Being Drunk

Trolleyed, bladdered, smashed, tanked up, hammered, tipsy, half cut, mashed, three sheets to the wind, puggled, scuttered, sloshed, wasted, plastered, maggoted, well oiled, spongy, ripped, pickled, wrecked, inebriated, merry, on a bender, had a skinfull, blotto, welly'd, stocious and totalled.

A Brief History of Beer

Beer brewing is probably the second oldest profession in the world. It started somewhere in Sumeria and Egypt in 6,000BC, from where it was carried to Europe by the Romans. It subsequently spread via the monks and their monasteries, abbeys, and mission stations across northern Europe.

In the past, people were literally "born into beer" because it was the safest source of clean water right up until the 19th century. Hops weren't introduced to the United Kingdom until around AD1400, although evidence shows that they were definitely in use in Germany and the Netherlands by AD800. Disciples of the hop, turn away now, because beer was made with adjuncts long before the hop took off. There are copious ancient recipes that include ingredients as diverse as heather, bog myrtle, cilantro (coriander), and tej (an Ethiopian mead or honey wine.) It has always been about experimenting and developing beer from the local ingredients available at the time.

If some brewers think of themselves today as a touch hardcore, spare a thought for King Wenceslas of Bohemia (1205–1253) who not only acted as God's representative on earth in order to repeal a law banning brewing in the 13th century, but also issued the death penalty to anyone caught exporting his beloved hops.

In 1516 William IV of Bavaria (1493–1550) became the world's first Environmental Health Officer when he introduced the very first food regulation—the Reinheitsdebot (more commonly known as the Bavarian/German Purity Law.) This ordered that beer could only be made from water, barley, and hops.

Sam Whitbread III (1830–1915) is credited with having pioneered the greatest improvement in brewing history when he brought Louis Pasteur to Britain in the 18th century. Pasteur's knowledge of yeast strains (and how to control them with temperature) led to beer being brewed all yearround, with greater consistency and fewer accidents. Only a few years earlier, a dozen or so people had been killed in the East End of London when some brewing vats exploded.

The Industrial Revolution and the rise of the British Empire saw the British expand their beer production and export sales across the globe—the India Pale Ales (IPAs) being the best example. This now classic style was the catalyst that triggered the northern brewers of Germany and Holland to start moving away from their old, dark-beer roots and pioneer the styles that we now associate with bottom-fermented lagers. The British and their success with IPAs was soon eclipsed by brewers in the United States, who quickly rose to prominence and dominance, conquering all predecessors in market share if not necessarily in taste at this point.

Modern beer

By 1989 (while I was pretending to be the next Salvador Dalí), very few pubs in England sold anything other than the mainstream, multi-national brands of homogenous lager—sold on strength and refrigerated to such an extent as to remove the likelihood of tasting anything. Fast-forward 20 years and I am now a publican in London, with two award-winning, cask-ale-driven pubs. In the United Kingdom, lager has been in decline by some 25 per cent over the last five years with real ale being the only driver in the sector. Microbreweries have prospered since the Beer Orders of 1989, when Margaret Thatcher benevolently attempted to break up the power of the "Big Six" brewers.

Some good has come of this, however; namely, the increase in the number of microbrewers. Their numbers have risen sharply from around 252 in 1989 to about 848 today, with another four opening in London in the last year alone, thus bringing the number in the capital to 20. I know of at least another two in the pipeline—and nearly all of these microbrewers will have had humble beginnings as homebrewers.

The United States pre-empted this revolution, with microbrewers starting to emerge when canny operators spotted that the public were tired of what they were being offered by the giant

Beer Facts from History

Medieval monks were convinced that the mortar for building churches was stronger mixed with ale rather than water.

Travelers in England are still entitled to claim ale and bread if they visit certain churches.

The Domesday Book (1086) records that the monks of St Paul's Cathedral in London brewed almost 70,000 UK gallons (84,000 US gallons) of ale that year.

Monks used the symbols X, XX, and XXX as symbols for the quality level of beer.

Through the Assize of Ale in 1266, ale-conners were appointed in UK boroughs and cities to test the quality of the ale and the accuracy of the measures being used.

By the early 14th century there was one "brewpub" for every 12 people in England.

Henry VIII gave the pint measurement its government stamp and inflicted the regulatory quagmire that is more commonly known in the United Kingdom today as Trading Standards.

Not so long ago—1810 to be precise—there were 48,000 alehouses for some eight million people in the UK. So, that's a pub for every 166 people. Where did it all go wrong?

John Wagner was the first to brew lager in North America. The year was 1840; the place was Philadelphia.

corporates. Brewers such as Samuel Adams, Sierra Nevada, Geary's, Stone, and Dogfish Head have all exploded flavor options onto a market literally gagging for something new and different. One could be forgiven for suspecting that Dogfish Head and Stone may be the inspiration behind the self-acclaimed Punk-brewers, BrewDog in Scotland.

The Brewing Process

If there is anything that embodies the punk-band, "anyone-can-have-a-go" spirit of the 1980s, it is micro- or homebrewing. As I have said, it is in essence a relatively simple process to master.

When you design and make a beer it will be a reflection of you and how you were feeling at the time. Depending on that moment, it could be grossly scientific, obliging, innovative, and experimental, or profoundly personal. The deep-seated satisfaction of having created your own beer—a project undertaken from start to finish—is a constant joy. You can brew beer at home using a kit, malt extract, or the full-mash method.

From a kit

Beer-making kits have come a long way from the early insipid kits of the 1970s and 1980s with their extravagant claims. The choice is now massive, with regional and global brands widely available. They are worlds apart scientifically from their bell-bottomed cousins and impart confidence in people because they brew with consistent results and quality. This is the simplest method and all you have to do is what it says on the can.

From malt extract

The next step up, this method uses ready-prepared liquid malt extract as its base—simply add your choice of hops, adjuncts, and yeast. Additional malt grains can also be added, if you wish. This is probably the most popular method in the United States. It's commonly done on the stove (although your partner may not thank you for this) with a medium-sized pot, gives you a jump time-wise on the all-grain method, and is easier to cool down. Furthermore, can sizes in multiples of 1.5kg (3¼ lb) can assist in scaling down recipes if storage and/or time are an issue. It is, however, two to three times more expensive than using the all-grain method. (This method is covered well in practically every American book on homebrewing, as well as on the Internet.)

From the all-grain, full-mash, traditional method (The Daddy!)

For me, this is the way to go if you are serious about wanting to brew great-tasting beer that either replicates your favorites as much as possible or pushes the boundaries of beer boredom. It will cost you more in time and equipment, but with a bit of practice you will quickly be able to design and adapt beers to your own exacting requirements. The rewards will be deeply satisfying and hopefully soften the cost of the extra kit!

So, cut your teeth and master the traditional process. Don't be shy—the old adage that you learn from your mistakes is true. Be patient, and if you're worried about the brew not working out, scale down the ingredients. Do your apprenticeship for, say, five months and then it really is time to explore possibilities with other ingredients and techniques. You will progress from making good beer to great beer, I promise.

The three main concerns

When brewing beer at home, please bear the following points in mind because they can really have an impact on your chances of success.

Cleanliness Keep everything scrupulously clean if you want your beer to taste like something you'd drink rather than chuck on your fries (see page 24 for guidance on cleaning and sterilizing).

Water A 4% ABV beer is roughly 96% water. How hard or soft your water supply is will have a massive impact on the taste of your chosen beer style. Either way, start with your faucet (tap) supply until you are more confident. If you are concerned about calcium and other chemical treatments, either filter or boil the water for 15–20 minutes. Gypsum salts (among other things) are often used by brewers to treat water. Treatment packs are available from your local homebrew store and you can play around endlessly with this aspect of homebrewing (see pages 45–46).

Homebrewing Five Steps to Success

When brewing beer at home, you will be following these stages:

1. Malted barley is soaked in hot water (liquor) to extract the malt sugars that it contains.

2. This malt-sugar solution is boiled with hops.

3. The malt-hop infusion is cooled and yeast pitched to start fermentation.

4. The yeast ferments and eats the sugars, burping out carbon dioxide (CO_2) and ethyl alcohol.

5. Once the fermentation is complete, the beer can be bottled, kegged, or casked with a small amount of priming sugar to create some secondary fermentation and thus natural carbonation.

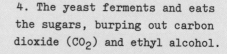

Storage How do you want to store your beer? In demijohns, poly-pins, mini-pins, barrels (firkins), kegs, or bottles? Unless exceptionally conditioned, beer in larger containers will tend to be less carbonated. Beer that is secondarily fermented in bottles will last longer, but will display different flavor notes and textures.

The six degrees

The mash, the sparge, the boil, fermentation, racking, and conditioning, and, oh yes, the best bit—the drinking. Oh, that's seven. No wonder I'm a publican! Seriously, though, you will need to master the following six key stages in order to produce beer that you will enjoy drinking.

1. The Mash This is where you create your brewing wort by converting malt starch from grain into sugars. This is done by soaking the grain in heated water at about 68°C (154°F). I prefer to use an insulated mash tun with a hop strainer, but a basic bucket lined with a clean grain sack to create a giant tea bag will also do. The term "mash" is quite literal; you add the grain slowly to the pre-heated water (taken from your boiler) and stir, making sure that there is no dry grain. (Just like making creamy mashed potato, although your mash will look like porridge.)

Don't overdo it, though; too much stirring may result in cloudy beer because you will inevitably release too much starch, something the brewers of old didn't know. You want the grain hydrated but not saturated to the point of being waterlogged.

The temperature now needs to be maintained at 60–68°C (140–154°F). I prefer 66°C (151°F) for anything between 60–90 minutes. To adjust the temperature, just add hot or cold water accordingly. Like all good cooks, keep some pre-cooled and boiling water to hand.

2. The Sparge This is a Scottish invention, which, as you may imagine, was designed as the most efficient method of rinsing out as much of the converted sugars from the spent grain into the liquor to create the brewing wort. After draining off the majority of sweet malt liquor from the mash, we sparge by sprinkling water at a temperature of 75–80°C (167–175°F) over the surface of the mashed grain in order to extract as much malt sugar as possible and stop the sugar conversion. Please do not attempt any more stirring!

Pour the first and second draining back over the grain and top up with any spare liquor until the liquid is no longer sweet. The finger-licking test is adequate here (i.e. stick your finger under the faucet (tap) and lick it to see if the liquor is still sweet.) Once it isn't, turn off the tap. These run-offs are known as "runnings." Take your time here because you want lots of lovely fermentable sugars.

When doing this, be careful not to disturb the base grain bed because you do not want to draw off too much sediment. You can use a purpose-made sparger, a sanitized watering can, or a simple jug, just as long as you spread the liquor evenly over the grain surface. Let the liquor settle for around 10 minutes between each running, and don't pour in so much that it sits on the top of the grain. Don't squeeze your grain bag if you are using this method for mashing! Any spare liquor can be added to the boil as a top-up to that lost through evaporation.

3. The Boil Breweries conduct a boil in a copper, which, like a lot of brewing jargon, can be confusing, so beware. At home, the only difference between the all-grain and malt-extract methods is that for malt extract you can use a large pot on the stove instead of a cumbersome but dedicated gas or electric boiler.

Large, all-grain boilers for use with gas will help bring the brew up to temperature faster, and are more easily adjustable. Electric, kettle-like boiler elements have a habit of overheating and switching off. This is often due to hops clinging to the elements. Protect them with mesh or gauze or, better still, just stick with gas (although Burco boilers have concealed elements). Don't forget to consider how you will cool the resultant boil down to 20°C (68°F). I recently upgraded to a 55-litre (12-gallon/14½-US-gallon) boiler, which was, of course, too big for a bath of ice. Homebrewers used to allow the boil to cool over night. Alternatively, you can rig up a cooling element, which is readily available from homebrew stores.

4. Primary Fermentation This is the process of adding or pitching your yeast to convert the sugars in the brewing wort into alcohol and carbon dioxide. There are a wide variety of brewer's yeasts available and they come either dry or wet. You can, of course, cultivate yeast from beer bottles or from the cask beer at your local pub, which is especially useful if you are trying to clone/replicate your favorite beer (see page 49). Yeast cultivation is also explained in more depth on these pages. For sheer convenience and speed, I prefer the reliability of "smack-pack" yeasts, which are readily available online or from your local brew store.

5. Racking This is brewer-speak for transferring the beer after primary fermentation is completed into your desired choice of container. Whether you decide to use bottles, barrels, pins, mini-pins, or demijohns in order to "rack" your beer, it is crucial to consider where you will conduct this part of the gig. It must be sterile or you risk spoiling the beer. You need the fermenter to be above the receptacle of choice by a good 30cm (12in) to ensure gravity helps the flow rate. It's a good idea to move the container into place a couple of hours before siphoning in order to let any sediment drop to the bottom. It will improve your chances of "bright" beer (of course, if sediment is your thing, don't bother), as will skimming off any yeast from the surface.

Mixing the water and malt

The brewing wort

Preparing for sparging

Get a siphon with a faucet (tap) on the end so that you can control the flow-rate going into the container. One with a U-tube configuration at one end will help stop any sediment getting sucked along. Traditionally, you would have to place the U-tube in the bin, open the tap, and suck on it to the get beer through. This is fine if it's just you drinking the beer, but I recommend using a fermenter container with a tap at the bottom if you plan to move on commercially, or share with friends. Remember that there can be a great many germs in your mouth, so you need to keep everything as clean as possible. Lactobacilli are the most common beer-wreckers, with wild yeasts close behind, so try to keep spills to a minimum because this is the ideal opportunity for it to spread. Run your siphon into a pitcher (jug) first to minimize any spillages.

6. Conditioning Conditioning is the secondary fermentation that occurs in your chosen container, producing the carbon dioxide gas that gives beer its sparkle or slight fizz. For the purposes of secondary fermentation, I believe cask ale is king. It has a more rounded, fuller flavor that just can't be replicated by draught, bottling, or even bottle conditioning due to the "live" secondary fermentation and liberal dry hopping. The diversity and complexity of flavors paired with the uniqueness of cask is a great selling point for beers produced in the United Kingdom.

A vital part of the craft, a publican will mature a cask in the cellar. Although you can also do this, you'll have to drink it within three to five days once beer has been drawn off (36-pint pins are ideal). Depending on how "au naturel" you want your beer—and if you can contain your excitement—you can just container the beer and leave it for another couple of weeks to "condition" for the same effect. Any residual sugars will be enough to start a secondary ferment as long as the container is properly sealed.

So, only add as much priming sugar as is absolutely necessary, as per the manufacturer's instructions. The sugar feeds the remaining yeast, creating carbon dioxide. Put in too much and you get exceptionally frothy beer or—in the case of bottles—exploding glass.

If you use sugar, add roughly half a teaspoon to every 500ml (18 fl oz) of beer. Leave approximately 2.5cm (1in) of space at the top of the bottle when you are filling it and then cap as per the manufacturer's instructions. When you are satisfied that your containers are all tightly capped or barrel-sealed, keep in a warm place for a week at 20°C (68°F). Wipe down with sanitizer to get rid of any splashed beer. Then move them on to a cellar or adapted fridge for a couple of days at 12–15°C (54–60°F). Any yeast produced by the secondary fermentation will help "drop" the beer "bright" if the beer is kept cool. If you aren't worried about clarity, then go with it.

7. Lucky seven—drinking! Sample your beer after a week or so. If it is too "flat," move it back to a warm place and try again in a few days. If it is too lively, try chilling it before you pour it. If the beer is below 10°C (50°F), it is likely to suffer "chill haze;" if above 15°C (60°F), it is less likely to settle and drop "bright."

More yeast will be created during the secondary fermentation, so, in the case of bottles, try not to disturb it when pouring the beer into your glass. If the beer gushes, it is either highly conditioned or too warm. If it's the former, then happy days—just give it a couple more days to settle. If it's the latter, cool it down fast! Top-pressure and cask-breathers may assist, but keep this quiet from your beer-head mates.

Pouring and tasting your beer

I'm not going to insult your intelligence. If you don't know how to pour beer by now, ask your mother. If, on tasting, you find your beer hasn't turned out as you wanted, don't be disheartened. There are so many variables when brewing beer. At this level no two batches will be the same and things inevitably go wrong. Regional brewers and microbrewers often have to pour beer down the drain in pursuit of perfection. Start small until you have gained confidence.

A note on lagering

The process for brewing lager is exactly the same as for ale, except that lager is fermented at a much lower temperature (0–5°C/32–41°F) and ideally needs different yeasts. The primary fermentation takes twice as long and the finished article then needs to be stored for weeks, sometimes months, to properly "lager" (which is German for "store.") This is why it is beyond most homebrewers. Give it a go, though; I am sure that you will be able to brew something fairly flavorsome.

Essential Equipment

Aeration kit Consisting of a pump, filter, diffusion stone, and tubing, this important piece of kit introduces the oxygen to the wort that is necessary for the yeast to start the fermentation process.

Airlocks These are simple to use and make it easy to check whether your beer is producing CO_2. Look at the water line to see if the gas is bubbling through.

Aluminum (aluminium) stock pots These can be used instead of the mash tun for mashing, although this method is a little more tricky and, for the sake of a small investment, I would not want to recommend that someone try to strain the boiling mash, especially considering that you may well be lifting huge pots of boiling hot malt and water.

Boiler A large vessel (heated using gas or electricity) that holds a large volume of liquid, keeping it at the boil for the required time.

Bottles Any shape of bottle is fine, but make sure that you don't use a screw or twist-off cap. Bottles also need to be brown. (If you can get hold of swing-top bottles, then you will not need to get a bottle capper.)

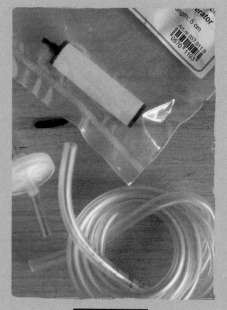

Aeration kit

Bottle capper A bench-crown capper is the easiest to use because it is fixed to your worktop surface, although two-handed cappers are more common. Both types of bottle capper can be found on homebrewing supply websites or in your local homebrew store.

Bottle dryer Holding 45–80 bottles, a bottle dryer or tree enables you to keep drying bottles clean.

Bottle filler A great gadget, although not essential, a bottle filler takes the place of a hose clamp for bottling your beer. Attach to one end of the siphon tubing. When the end of the wand hits the bottom of the bottle, a valve opens and lets the beer flow through.

Brushes A must-have for thoroughly cleaning tubing, airlocks, and fermenter necks. Ideally, you will need a carboy brush, pipe cleaners, and a narrow nylon brush. All available from homebrew stores.

Boiler

Bottle capper

Fermentation vessels

Mash tun

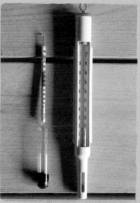
Original gravity reader
and thermometer

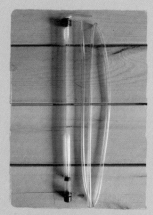
Tubing for bottling

Bucket For sterilizing all of your equipment. It needs to be big enough to hold a couple of gallons of sanitizer and your equipment.

Fermentation vessels Glass or plastic carboys or demijohns can be used for primary or secondary fermentation. If using for primary fermentation, use an airlock/blow-off valve as well. Also refers to large, food-grade, plastic fermentation vessels with an airtight lid suitable for attaching a bung and airlock/blow-off valve. Ideal for secondary fermentation.

Fermenting buckets Use food-grade buckets (capacity 25 litres/5½ gallons/6½ US gallons) with tight-fitting lids for primary fermentation. Try to get buckets with a tap fitted for ease of use. They should be easily obtainable from all good homebrew stores.

Grain bag A large, very fine mesh bag required for holding all of the grain during the mash. Always use a nylon bag as these are usually finer meshed and will last a lot longer than the muslin variety. The finer the mash, the fewer particles are left in the wort. The grain bag will need to measure at least 50 x 50cm (20 x 20in).

Hose clamp A device that is useful for opening and closing tubing while bottling. Always make sure that the clamp can click completely shut and fits the tubing.

Hydrometer and tube This is an inexpensive but essential piece of a homebrewer's kit. Hydrometers are calibrated at 15°C (60°F) and 20°C (70°F). If possible, buy one combined with a thermometer and calibrated to 20°C (70°F), enabling you to avoid having to use temperature adjustment charts. To calculate a rough Alcohol By Volume (ABV), subtract the Final Gravity (FG) from the Original Gravity (OG) and divide by 7.56. For example:

OG 1056 - FG 1010 = 46 (÷ 7.56 = 6% ABV)

Kegs I like the bottom-tap keg that holds around 26 litres (5½ gallons/6½ US gallons) and has a 10cm (4in) neck opening—it's easy to clean. The screw cap carries a pressure release and a CO_2 introduction valve to enable excess gas from over-priming to be released automatically. Additional gas can also be introduced to keep up internal pressure. A great keg especially if a brew needs time to mature and clear.

Mash paddle A device essential for mixing in the strike water and breaking up dough balls (dry pockets of malt) during the mashing process. A mash paddle is a basic piece of brewing equipment, and it is difficult to do all-grain brewing without one. Most real homebrew enthusiasts will craft their own brew paddle from oak or maple, but never use pine as this will impair the flavor of the beer. It will need to be fairly long and the base oblong in shape with six to eight large holes drilled into it. If you are making your own paddle, fill the pot a gallon at a time and mark the volumes on the paddle in gallon increments. You'll then be able to see roughly how much wort you have at any one time.

Mash tun These are easy to get hold of through the Internet or a homebrew store. They take a lot of the pain out of boiling up malt on your stove and the inevitable sticky boil-overs that happen. Mash tuns are highly efficient and capable of mashing up to 10kg (22lb) of grain. They usually come complete with tap and integral wort separator and with a capacity of 30 litres (6½ gallons/8 US gallons).

Racking cane An essential bit of kit for siphoning beer into bottles, usually long enough to fit 23-litre (5-gallon/6-US-gallon) fermenters. I opt for the plastic variety, but metal ones are also available. Also, any residue is easier to detect in the clear plastic types. There are some with a built-in suction chamber that can start a siphon without you having to suck on the tube and, as we have pointed out elsewhere, earlier sanitation is key, so it is not a great idea to introduce bacteria at this point.

Scales (digital) I cannot stress enough the importance of buying a set of scales that will measure kilograms and grams. Once you have bought your full list of grain, hops and adjuncts, you will not want to waste a single gram, so do yourself a favor and invest in a set of digital scales!

Strainer A normal fine-meshed sieve works well and is used to strain out the trub. I use a metal sieve.

Temperature controller If you would like to go all out, pick up an old refrigerator and keep it solely for your lager development; all you need to do is plug the fridge into the controller and plug the controller into the wall. Fix the built-in thermometer in the fridge and set the controller to a lagering temperature of 13°C (55°F) for primary and 4°C (40°F) for secondary fermentation (usually one month). The controller will do its thing, and turn off and on as needed to achieve and maintain the correct temperature.

Thermometer If you can't get hold of a combined hydrometer/ thermometer, then a metal thermometer will do. Don't be tempted to buy a glass one as they break fairly easily.

Tubing You will need food-grade vinyl tubing, which can be seen through. The tubing should ideally be thrown away after 10 brews and new ones bought. You will need a wide tube to use as a blow-off hose and a narrow one which will be connected to your racking cane. Any good homebrew store will be able to advise you on this. (Wide tubing should be approximately 2.5cm/1in inside diameter and narrow tubing 1cm/⅜in inside diameter.)

Turkey baster Great for obtaining small samples to taste or to use as samples to find your specific gravity.

CLEANING KIT

To make great beer, clean and sanitize obsessively. Make sure you have a sterilizing bucket, some sterilizing chemicals (for making up a sanitizing solution,) a dish-cloth, and a spritzer bottle.

Sterilization

If you are serious about making really great beer, then read on. What you learn here will make all the difference between having drinkable beer and pouring it directly down the drain. Sanitize, sanitize, and then sanitize again; boring this may be, but you will thank me later!

Make up a solution of sanitizer in a bucket and submerge all of your brewing equipment. Sanitizing solution can be obtained from your homebrew store, whether you opt for a liquid or a powder. I personally prefer a chlorine-based powder. Just follow the manufacturer's instructions. Then, put some sanitizing solution into a spritzer so that you can clean

worktops and do any last-minute sanitation jobs. Keep a dish-cloth solely for beer-making and don't use your usual kitchen one because this will contain incalculable numbers of beer-destroying bacteria.

Anything that is alive and thriving

Water treatment chemicals

Sterilizing equipment before use

Sterilizing with boiling water

before the boil will be dead afterward, so don't become obsessive before the main event. At this stage, all of the equipment just needs to be clean—after the boil is when problems can occur. After the boil everything that comes into contact with the beer needs to be sterilized; that is, everything including the fermenting buckets, tubing, and valves need to have been soaked in the sterilizing solution. If you follow the advice above, then the outcome is potentially going to be a good one. Good luck!

Essential Ingredients

In my book, the saying "you are what you eat" is bang on. So, using the best ingredients when brewing beer is vital to success—always try to eliminate as many areas as possible where you might slip up. Wherever I can, I opt for organic ingredients.

Water

This can be a hugely complex subject. While there is no doubt that good brewing liquor improves the extraction of malt sugars, enhances hop utilization, and gives a better chance of a cleaner ferment, it must be remembered that for hundreds of years brewers made perfectly good beers with no water treatment other than boiling.

Much is made of the generally accepted belief that Burton water is the best brewing water in the world. This myth has been exposed by the great beer writer of our times, Roger Protz, who recently unearthed public supply charts dating back to the height of IPA fame that appear to dispel the claims for Burton. The charts show great variation in carbonates, suggesting that the so-called naturally occurring gypsous water was not as idyllic as the marketing would suggest. Today's public supply charts show an alarming disparity between day and night. At night there is a high nitrate and sodium ion concentration. Taking this into account, you may want to consider using your mains water supply during the day when nitrate levels are lower, as these will batter your yeast and affect your end results.

Water is all too often overlooked by home brewers, but the liquor's impact on your brew cannot be denied. This is mainly due to the levels of calcium carbonate, sodium, and nitrates that may be present. With brew science having come on so much in the last 10 years, technology and the improved quality of ingredients really do give us the ability to produce beer on a level playing field with our commercial cousins. So, it would be shame not to nail the last piece of the jigsaw into place by failing to consider the water used for your brewing liquor.

Before letting this descend into a chemistry lesson, I would suggest fitting a good filter to your mains supply, such as the FilterStream by SodaStream. This removes chlorine, polyphenols, and heavy metals, etc. No plumbing is required, either; just replace the cartridges as per the manufacturer's instructions. Filtration is the easiest method by far and will also catch other nasties, such as rust and sand.

Alternatively, boil your water supply for 15–20 minutes to force out the suspended chemicals. You are aiming for a pH of around 5.3–5.6 for bottom-fermenting beers and 5.0–5.1 for top-fermenting ones. So, if you don't boil or filter, you will shove this up to something much higher. Don't forget to clean out your boiler afterward to remove the chemical scum and sediment (we don't want this reintroducing itself.)

If you fancy playing around with water quality, then turn to page 45 for the full-on, teacher bit on this fascinating subject. turn to page 45

Malt

Malt

The most popular grain used for beer production is barley, although wheat grain is also used, particularly in Belgian, Weiss, and Wit beers. Today, barley must exhibit a range of specialized properties in order to meet a

brewer's exacting standards. It is analyzed by variety and for nitrogen and moisture content before malting is even attempted. Barley is the most commonly malted grain due to the diastatic or "enzymatic power" of the grain. This generally refers only to malts—grains that have begun to germinate. The act of germination results in the production of a number of enzymes, such as amylase, which convert starch into sugar; thereby, sugars can be extracted from the barley's starches simply by soaking the grain in water at a controlled temperature. This is called mashing.

The grain's husk is incredibly hard, so malters have to add water, heat, and aeration to make the grain germinate. Once germinated, the growth is stopped there by a process called dry kilning, making it easier to develop the enzymes that convert the starches to sugars. This is also vital for the production of enzymes that break down protein for conversion to alcohol by yeast.

In general, the hotter a grain is kilned, the less its diastatic activity. Consequently, only lightly colored grains can be used as base malts (main malt), with Munich malt being the darkest base malt generally available. Once the malting of the grain has taken place, it can be roasted to produce varying levels of sweetness and color.

Malt grains have to be crushed for brewing purposes, but you can buy them uncrushed if you want to add more time to your craft. The most common base malt is pale malt or, in the case of lager, pale lager malt, which is sweet. In contrast, the crystal malt used in the production of British bitters will have been slightly roasted to produce a sweet, toffee-like flavor and a browner color.

The majority of brewers, commercial or otherwise, use pale malt as the main constituent of their grist. The grist or "grain bill" (which is also sometimes referred to as the mash roll) is the sum of malts, grains, and adjuncts that are put through the mash. The combination of these constituents will determine the color, malt flavor, and alcoholic strength of the beer.

Another general rule of thumb is that around 90 per cent of a grist will be pale malt—hence the term "base malt"—with only 10 per cent of specialty malts and adjuncts being added to vary the degree of color or flavor.

The color scale for malts is evaluated by the Standard Reference Method (SRM), Lovibond (°L), American Society of Brewing Chemists (ASBC), or European Brewery Convention (EBC) standards.

While SRM and ASBC originate in North America and EBC in Europe, all three systems can be found in use throughout the world. (See right for an example of a color-scale chart.)

Coloring malts are similar to base malts but have been kilned for longer. This gives them a darker color and a more distinct character. Examples of coloring malts include amber malt (60–100 EBC), brown malt (130–150 EBC), chocolate malt (500–1350 EBC), and black malt (1400–1600 EBC).

SRM/Lovibond	Example	Beer color	EBC
2	Pale lager		4
3	German Pilsener		6
4	Pilsner Urquell		8
6			12
8	Weissbier		16
10	Bass pale ale		20
13			26
17	Dark lager		33
20			39
24			47
29	Porter		57
35	Stout		69
40			79
70	Imperial stout		138

Malt range

Nothing but the best barley is used for malting. Once malted, the barley should still be sweet in taste and smell, as well as able to float in water. Malt is roasted light or dark, although you will find it sold with various descriptions and names as is shown in the malt chart on page 30. Do not be afraid to ask for advice at your local homebrew store if you are in any doubt about the best malt to use for a particular beer. However, bear in mind that the strength of the beer is imparted by pale malt (i.e. the base malt) because this gives the highest yield. Crystal and/or caramel malts will add depth and substance to sweeter beers, amber and brown malts will have a similar effect but, being slightly darker, will give a smoother finish and deeper color. Black malt is heavily roasted, delivering a very rich flavor that is particularly good for stouts and porters. Finally, roast barley, although not as rich as black malt, is needed to produce a dry finish to certain beers and dry stouts.

MALT CHART WORKING ACROSS THE CHART ARE THE VARIOUS NAMES FOR THE SAME MALT OR ADJUNCT.

2-rale	Pilsen	Lager			
Pale ale	Maris otter	Pearl			
Stout malt	Halcyon				
Ashburne	Mild ale	Vienna	Aromatic		
Bonlander	Munich	Munich I			
Vienna					
Munich 10	Munich	Munich II	Dark Munich		
Dextrine	Carafoam				
Victory	Amber	Melanoidin	Biscuit	Kiln Amber	
Crystal 10	Caramalt	Carapils	Caramalt	Carahell	Light caramel
Crystal 20	Carared	Caravienne	Caramel Vienna		
Crystal 30	Pale crystal	Caramunich I	Carastan	Caramel amber	
Crystal 40	Crystal malt 40–50	Caramunich II	Carastan	Medium caramel	Caramel Munich 40
Crystal 60	Crystal malt 60–70	Caramunich III	Caramunich	Dark caramel	Caramel Munich 60
Crystal 80	Dark crystal malt	Crystal malt 85–95	Dark caramunich		

Crystal 90	Dark crystal				
Crystal 120	Dark crystal	Dark crystal II	Cararoama	Special B (118–124)	Caramel Munich 120
Special roast	Brown malt	Kiln Amber			
Extra special	Kiln coffee				
Pale chocolate	Carafa I				
Chocolate	Carafa II				
Black patent	Carafa III	Black malt	Roasted malt	Kiln black	
Roasted barley	Black barley				
Roasted wheat	Chocolate wheat				
Wheat					
Dark wheat					
Crystal wheat	Carawheat	Caramel wheat			
Roasted rye					
Rye malt					
Caramel rye malt					
Oat malt					
Peated malt	Smoked malt				

Malt range

Pale malt is dried at temperatures designed to preserve all the brewing enzymes in the grain. This keeps down the cost of kilning, making it the least expensive and most popular malt available (with the exception of lager malt).

Mild malt is mainly derived from Triumph barley and is commonly used in Europe for lager malt, as well as for milds in the United Kingdom. It is kilned slightly hotter than pale malt for a fuller, sweeter flavor.

Acid malt contains lactic acid, which will lower the pH of your mash, creating the same effect as adding gypsum to the liquor, but it is softer on the palate. It is normally used for making top-end lagers.

Pilsner malt is kilned slowly at low temperatures until dry and then toasted at 80°C (175°F). It is very pale, with a strong sweet flavor and high enzyme content, making it a good base malt. It is often added to pale beers for flavor and high yields.

Vienna malt is kilned at higher temperatures to Pilsner and is therefore darker and more aromatic. Also used as a base malt, it will add both color and flavor to Vienna and Marzen beer styles.

Munich malt is both darker and fuller flavored than Vienna. It has a high enzyme content despite its high-temperature kiln and is an essential ingredient for German bock beers.

Melanoidin malt from Bamberg, in Germany, has an aromatic, full flavor and is slightly lighter in color than crystal malt. It is used to make medium dark beers, particularly Munich lagers.

Crystal malt is a British variety. It can be pale or dark, but averages 150–160 EBC, provides a strong, nutty, caramel taste and adds depth to the flavor of the beer.

Honey malt is much like crystal malt, but softer on the palate due to its slightly lighter roasted overtone.

Stout malt is actually quite pale in spite of its name. A stout's color comes from roasted malt and usually roasted, unmalted barley.

Amber malt is a toasted form of pale malt, which is used with other malts due to its low enzyme content. You should use this for English brown ales, milds, and old ales.

Smoked malt originates from Germany and is popular in the production of Alt/Rauchbiers. It is usually smoked with beech, but there is a Scottish version that is smoked over peat. It is a powerful malt, so should be used sparingly.

Brown malt is not too dissimilar to smoked malt, and is used in dark ales.

Coffee malt will impart a distinctive coffee aroma, as its name suggests, so be very careful when choosing the quantity to use.

Black malt is kilned to a very high temperature, leaving it with no enzymes and less starch, and thus little fermentable extract. Very bitter, it is used for both flavor and color in dark beers.

Chocolate malt is similar to black malt but softer. It has a smoky rather than bitter flavor, has no enzymatic content and is used with roasted, unmalted barley in dark beers.

Adjuncts

These are those grains used in the grist that are not derived from malted barley. Unmalted grains are sometimes used, but these require mashing for over 90 minutes to extract the necessary sugars.

Roast Barley gives stout its burnt, bitter essence and ruby-black hue. It weighs in at 1600–1700 EBC, so, as you can imagine, it should be used sparingly or it will be an overpowering flavor in your beer.

Black barley is roasted to a greater degree than roast barley, which produces a pronounced and very strong burnt flavor and darker color.

Flaked barley offers a grainy flavor and helps with head retention. It can be used in large quantities for bitters and dark beers, but can cause haze problems in paler styles.

Torrified barley is made from heating barley kernels. With a distinctive flavor, it is also good for head retention.

Wheat malt

When flaked, wheat provides the protein haze characteristically common in Wheat/Weiss beers and is also used in British styles for head retention in which it can make up 50 per cent of a grain bill. Torrified wheat is used for a tighter, creamy head retention.

Flaked or torrified maize is commonly used by the British to lighten the color without changing the taste too much; think Stella Artois.

Rye will provide the very distinctive, spicy dryness associated with beer like the German Roggenbier. Like wheat, rye has no husk, and is difficult to malt, so doesn't form a filter bed in the mash.

Sorghum and millet are gluten-free grains popular in African and Indian brewing, often creating dark, hazy beers suitable for those allergic to gluten. I don't have any recipes for beer

associated with these grains, such as Chhaang, Pomba, or Namibian Oshikundu, so if you find any please forward them on!

Rice and corn are often used as substitutes for malt grain by commercial brewers. They are pretty flavorless, but a much cheaper way to replace malt or sugar in order to increase strength in a beer, but not the body. This "thinning out" was jumped on by the giants of the North American brewing industry to create a lager style now diametrically opposed to those of Germany or the Czech Republic.

Buckwheat and quinoa are not grains but do contain high enough levels of protein and starch without gluten to enable the production of beer suitable for those suffering from coeliac disease.

Weyermann malt of Bamberg offer a range of fantastic specialty malts as well as a decent range of organics.

Sugar

This should ideally come under the adjunct section, but, like all aspects of brewing, it can create a lengthy thesis. As we are trying not to go there, we will limit it to a few paragraphs.

Unlike the complex starches in malt, which need to be broken down into simpler forms through malting and mashing, sugars such as demerara are practically there already. They can be added to both the boil and the fermentation. How much you use will depend on the alcohol content and complexity that you require. Add too much, and you can end up with cider- or champagne-style dryness or a poorly balanced beer, so be careful.

Essentially—excluding extreme circumstances— you shouldn't be aiming to add more than 20 per cent in adjunct sugar above and beyond the malt sugar you have extracted from the grain. If you want a strong beer above 10% ABV, then add the sugar to the fermentation. Also, be careful to check your yeast spec to make sure that it won't be overcome by the adjunct and not ferment the beer properly. The later you add the sugars, the more aroma and flavor will be instilled in your beer. When adding sugars to the fermentation, sterilize them in hot water until they dissolve and allow to cool to 27°C (81°F) before adding to the fermenting beer. Roughly 500g (18oz) of sugar will add ten points or so to the original gravity.

You can use the following sugars: pure cane sugar, demerara sugar, Belgian amber candi sugar, dark brown sugar, Belgian light candi sugar, and light brown sugar.

Hops

Hops counterbalance the sweetness of malt. There are three main types: bittering hops (added at the start of the boil), aroma hops (added at the end of the boil,) and, of course, dual-purpose hops. Additionally, hops act as a great natural preservative. In fact, the combination of high hop rates together with high alcohol content created the antibiotic effect that allowed the first IPAs to survive the long journeys from Britain to India. In the United Kingdom there are approximately 18 indigenous varieties of hops.

The hop or *Humulus lupulus* (to use the botanical name) is a vigorous, climbing herbaceous perennial that will grow up to 5.4m (18ft) high if you let it. The female cones are more commonly used. It is a highly resinous plant related to hemp. The resins are made up of two main acids: alpha and beta. The alpha acid gives flavor and the beta acid provides aroma. Beta acids should nearly always be introduced toward the end of the boil as

over-oxidization can result in off-flavors akin to rotten vegetables or cooked corn. Dual-purpose hops have enough alpha acid for bitterness, but also enough essential oils to offer flavor and aroma. For increased flavor, add more hops in the middle, and for more aroma add more toward the end of the boil.

Noble hops are practically that of appellation/ designation, being Hallertau, Saaz, Spalt, and Tettnang. Lager traditionally contains these hops. English ales, on the other hand, use Fuggle, Golding, Target, Pioneer, or Progress. New World varieties popular with craft brewers today include Cascade, Citra, Chinook, Columbia, Mount Hood, Nelson Sauvin, and Willamette.

The supply of hops can be erratic, as the alpha acids and harvest vary naturally from year to year. If you can't get a certain type or the same AA (alpha acids) percentage, don't fret; simply substitute it with either a higher volume or a different variety. Happy Hops, Get Hoppy, and Brew Target are good app software that will remove the pain of working this out, but it's quite simple, so here's the equation for the calculation anyway:

New substitute hop weight =
recipe weight x AA% of recipe
divided by the new substitute hop AA

Higher-quality worts tend to utilize less bitterness, so you may need to up the quantity of hops. A rough guide is 10 per cent more boil hops for every ten points of original gravity over 1.060.

As you will see from the sample recipes, there are endless ways to promote more hops, even after the wort has boiled. This generally takes the form of "dry hopping" using pellets or whole-leaf hops as fermentation dies down or during the storage transfer. Hop-oil derivatives can also be added at

Brewing sugar

Hops

about 50mg (0.001oz) per 23 litres/5 gallons/6 US gallons) to significantly increase the hop profile, although the latter is frowned upon by many brewers.

Traditionally, brewers would use a bittering hop, possibly two, and one aroma hop. Today, as you will see, some brewers are using six hops or more for bittering, with more hops added halfway through for flavor, and numerous mixes of beta and dual-purpose hops at the end of the boil. There are no limits to the changes to what was once an accepted principle.

Once you build up a collection of hops, it may be advantageous to store them in a freezer. Don't buy hops in a transparent bag, but foil-wrapped instead to ensure freshness. UV light plays havoc with the hop oils, which is why brown bottles are used for storing beer. (For a full briefing chart on hops with descriptions, origins, and type, as well as suggested substitutes see pages 50–53.)

Yeast

Yeasts are largely forgotten about compared with the other main constituents of beer, perhaps because many don't think the choice of yeasts will change the flavor profile considerably. However, this is not true (although I have been somewhat guilty of this myself.) I recently attended an event held by Charles Faram and Wye Hops Ltd. (and sponsored by the National Hop Association of Britain,) where the same ale recipe was brewed using four different yeasts by Fermentis (yeast suppliers to the trade.) The resulting impact on flavor variation was shocking, particularly the one using T-58: it offered very strong, spicy, fruity, and woody notes to an ale—from a yeast usually associated with stouts and barley wine.

As a brewer you can still influence your beer at fermentation stage, depending on the yeast you select, the way you rehydrate it, how you pitch it, and at what temperature you do so (not forgetting

Yeast

Champagne yeast when you are halfway to your intended final gravity. In this way, the beer will retain more of the ale characteristics than the dryness associated with wine and cider.

Whichever yeast you choose, make sure you prepare it in advance because cooled wort is at high risk of infection and you don't want it standing around waiting to get spoilt. (For a more comprehensive guide to the different yeast types and how to use them, as well as advice on how to culture your own, see page 46.)

If you would like to clone or replicate a favorite beer (see page 49), you can culture the individual brewer's strain via a bottle of that beer or indeed a "green" and "undropped" barrel at your local pub. Dry yeasts used to receive a bad press because they picked up wild yeasts while going through the drying process, but technological improvements mean that this should no longer be a problem.

Personally, I love the WY Yeasts, especially the "smack-packs." They are more expensive but so convenient, and provide a great selection of specialty strains. Don't forget that your local commercial brewers may be willing to sell you their strain for a much lower rate. This goes for a lot of other ingredients, too!

whether you are using a fresh starter or a re-pitch.) When choosing a yeast, always consider the alcohol content. High levels of alcohol are toxic to yeast and can kill it, stopping further fermentation. Strong beers need a yeast with good apparent attenuation (AA), which is the posh word for the measurable amount of sugars that a yeast can eat. An average yeast will attenuate 65 to 75 per cent of the sugar suspended in the liquid. One solution is to pitch more or another type of yeast as fermentation is beginning to slow down, which helps to ferment higher-than-average sugar levels. An example would be to begin with an ale yeast for the first half of fermentation and then pitch a wine or

Fruits, herbs, and other things— spike it as you like it!

So, you've mastered the traditional principles, you are making consistent beer, are comfortable with the permutations, familiar with the varying styles, and know your palate. Now it's time to ignore convention and start being imaginative in your choice of additional ingredients. The possibilities are endless, from subtle changes with a Bock using lemongrass and galangal to Heffeweiss with blood orange or juniper.

Perceived wisdom has constraints, which will hold you back. Yes, Black IPA is not strictly an India Pale Ale, but by adding darker malts into the grist, some of the brewing guys (such as those at the Windsor & Eton Brewery, in England) are challenging tradition and creating a talking point. It may not be to a purist's taste but anything that promotes more talk about beer, pubs and the community is all good by me. Ask yourself, would the same critics of Black IPA have bemoaned the aggressive hopping rates of the original IPAs or do they cry about US Double IPAs?

You don't have to be quirky to change a dynamic within a recipe. At the same time, testing yourself will not only improve your knowledge of how and why certain ingredients affect the final outcome, but it may also lead to some damn-fine nirvana. Remember using fruits, flowers, and herbs is not a new thing. Historically, beers were flavored with virtually anything to hand long before the use of hops. Williams Bros of Alloa, in Scotland, have been going since 1993. Having researched some indigenous historic recipes, they created some esoteric gems, such as Heather Fraoch and Kelpie Seaweed Ale. Similarly, young and emerging brewers continue to experiment. Ones to watch in the United Kingdom, for example, are Brodies, Dark Star, Downton, Kernel, Saltaire, and Thornbridge.

Woodchips The effect that woodchips have on flavor has been well known throughout the brewing industry for many years. Using woodchips can impart a desirable flavor characteristic that is not found in beers brewed using normal methods. Ideally, the woodchips will be from oak. They are normally toasted and can then be soaked in whisky, brandy, or any other liquor that you feel brave enough to try. You will need to soak the woodchips for at least 2 weeks prior to brewing. The woodchips can be added directly to the hot wort and then removed with the trub.

Some herbs, flowers, and spices used in brewing

Bitter orange

Blackberries

Blood orange

Cardamom

Chamomile

Cherries

Chilies

Chocolate nibs

Cilantro (coriander)

Cinnamon

Citrus fruit peel

Cloves

Cocoa

Elderflowers

Fennel seed

Figs

Ginger

Ground coffee

Heather

Hibiscus flowers

Juniper

Lavender

Lemon verbena

Lemongrass

Nutmeg

Passion fruits

Peaches

Raspberries

Rose hips

Saffron

Sarsaparilla

Strawberries

Beer-flavoring orange peel

The Basic Method

Producing beer from a full mash requires care and skill, which comes with time and patience. Homebrewing this way can potentially produce the best beer that you've ever tasted.

Before you start

To make a 20-litre/4½-gallon/5-US-gallon batch, in total you will need approximately 25–30 litres/ 5½–6½ gallons/6½–8 US gallons of water prior to boil/chemical treatment, as you will lose volume at nearly all major stages, such as calcium boil off, grain absorption, wort boil, hop absorption, etc. How much you lose in evaporation will vary massively according to the size of your boiler, how vigorously you boil, and time spent boiling. In the book's "basic method," we state around 10 litres/ 2¼ gallons/2½ US gallons for mash and the same again for sparge, so once you have treated your 25–30 litres/5½–6½ gallons/6½–8 US gallons either by boiling or chemical treatment, anything in excess of 20 litres/4½ gallons/5 US gallons can be set aside and cooled. This excess can be used to "top up" as per step 15 and/or added to the sparge.

The Mash

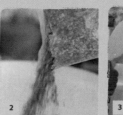

1 Heat 20 litres/4½ gallons/5 US gallons of water to 72–75°C (162–167°F) in your boiler.

2 Weigh the malt and other constituents of the "grain grist" or mash roll ready for putting in the mash tun.

3 Use a large measuring jug to remove 10 litres/2¼ gallons/ 2½ US gallons of boiler water for pouring into the mash tun.

4 Pour water into the mash tun to heat it. With a thermometer, check the water temperature is 72–75°C (162–167°F). Add hot or cold water to adjust the temperature as necessary.

5 Add the grain grist to the water in the mash tun. Stir the grain grist gently into the water, making sure that there are no dry lumps of grain, until you have a porridge-like substance.

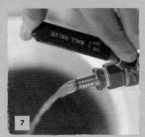

6 After stirring, the temperature should fall to 65–68°C (149–154°F). Allow to stand, covered, for 60–90 minutes (see individual recipes for the mashing time.)

7 Drain the mash tun slowly into a bucket or fermenting bin for 10 minutes. Don't allow it to run dry or you will end up with a set mash. Pour this back in and repeat.

The Sparge

8 Pour the wort into a watering can ready for sparging. Start the sparge with about the same amount of water that you used for the mash (i.e. 10 litres/2¼ gallons/2½ US gallons) at a temperature of 75–80°C (167–175°F).

9 When sparging, go slowly and don't allow water to sit on top of the grain. Let it all drain through before adding the next load. Repeat as necessary. Remember, you will need approximately the same amount of water for the sparge as you did for the mash. This will be your brewing wort.

The Boil

10 Place the hop strainer in the boiler to create your copper before transferring the wort. If you don't, the tap will get blocked with hops and removing it will stir cloudy proteins around your beer. Transfer the wort into the copper and turn up the heat until it comes to the boil.

11 Now chuck in your bittering hops (see page 34) and be as rough as you like with the stirring. Don't forget to take in a draw on that aroma. Keep the heat at a rolling boil (not a simmer) for an hour or so.

12 Copper finings are usually added 15 minutes from the end of the boil or as per manufacturer's instructions to "drop" your beer "bright". Irish moss, which is derived from seaweed, is the most common choice of fining, while Protofloc is a popular brand. Gelatin is also used by some brewers. All these finings are available online or from a local homebrew store. After the secondary fermentation, brewers use isinglass/sturgeon fish gut, which acts as a magnet to pull cloud-creating particles down to the bottom, thus "dropping" the beer "bright" and clear. Isinglass may be obtainable, as might yeast, from your local microbrewery or good real-ale pub.

13 Turn off the heat and add the aroma hops (or as directed by the recipe). After 5–10 minutes, stir and leave to soak. After 20 minutes, stir again and repeat once more after another 20 minutes or so.

14 If you haven't been clean so far, now you have to be! Drain the copper to allow the hopped wort infusion to flow into the fermenting bin, or carboy, leaving behind the strained hops that haven't blocked your tap (you clever thing you!)

15 Adjust the volume to 23 litres/5 gallons/ 6 US gallons with cold water, then cover, and cool to about 20°C (68°F). This can be done in a bath filled with ice-laden water or with a cooling element from a homebrew store. Carboys are great if you are planning to bottle your beer because they save time by allowing you to add priming sugar in one go, rather than individually to each bottle. They also allow you to see clearly how well the yeast is performing.

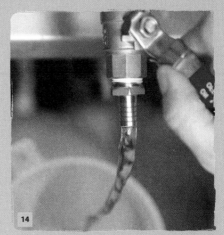

Fermentation

16 Use a sterilized container to mix the yeast with some sterile water or wort, ready for pitching it into the fermenter. You can store any remaining yeast in the fridge for your next brew (but for no longer than a week.)

17 Ideally, check the original gravity of the wort with a hydrometer. You will need to cool a sample of wort down to 20°C (68°F) to do this. Most hydrometers are calibrated at this temperature, so check you are reading 20°C (68°F).

18 When the wort is between 20–30°C (68–86°F), pitch your chosen yeast to ferment. Whatever yeast you use, it is vital to get it going well to prevent any possible infection, so give the wort a good rouse or stir to introduce oxygen to the beer and assist the yeast's consumption of those lovely fermentable sugars.

19 Now cover the fermenter with its sterilized lid, bung and airlock, and then store at 18–20°C (65–68°F) to ensure proper fermentation.

20 After 3–5 days, check and record the original gravity with the hydrometer. This will help you spot if things aren't going to plan. A good hydrometer will have a useful

little colored band to help you identify when the gravity has fallen to around 1010, thus telling you that it is time to rack your beer. Alternatively, when the gravity has remained static for 2 consecutive days, it is usually done – this will be the final gravity. Bang tidy!

How to Use the Recipes in this Book

Original Gravity	1047

(This refers to the weight of the beer before fermentation)

Water	23 litres/5 gallons/6 US gallons

(The amount of water that you will need for mashing and sparging)

Mash Roll	Weight
Pale ale malt	4.9kg (10¾ lb)
Crystal malt	200g (7oz)
Chocolate malt	45g (1½ oz)

(The mixture of grains required to make up the "grain bill" or "mash roll" for mashing)

Mash Schedule	1 hour

(The amount of time you will need to leave your mash roll in the mash tun)

In the Boil	Weight	Time
UK Challenger	22g (¾ oz)	90 minutes
UK Bramling Cross	20g (¾ oz)	20 minutes from end
UK Fuggles	16g (½ oz)	5 minutes from end
Protofloc/Irish moss	1 teaspoon	15 minutes from end

(Provides the list of hop types, adjuncts, and finings you will need to boil up in the brewing wort)

Boil duration	1½ hours

(The amount of time for which you will need to boil the hops and other ingredients in the brewing wort)

Yeast	London ale yeast — WY-1318

(Provides the amount and recommended type of yeast for the particular beer)

Target FG	1012

(This is the final gravity and refers to the weight of the beer after fermentation)

Target ABV	4.6%

(Indicates the alcoholic strength of the beer)

A Little More Brew Science...

Although homebrewing beer is essentially a simple, step-by-step process, there is a certain amount of science involved in it. Although you may think that the scientific explanations will be rather dull, reading through this next section should give you the knowledge to make your homebrewing more interesting.

Water

Before you start experimenting with this, it is worth contacting your local water board and requesting a full alkalinity analysis of your water in ppm (parts per million.) In general, calcium carbonate is added to make dark beer from soft water and to help balance the roasted grain's natural acidity, whereas calcium chloride and calcium sulphate (gypsum) are used to lower the pH and thereby increase acidity. Most water supplies have too much carbonate and not enough calcium for brewing pale ales and bitter.

Brupaks' CRS (Carbonate Reducing Solution) and DLS (Dry Liquor Salts) are great products but, as with most things, there is an endless supply of products available that perform the same function. For lager, some recommend using CRS in the mash liquor with lactic acid added to the mash tun to lower the pH. For the purist, a specialist German acid malt can be added to the grist to achieve the same effect.

Yeasts—culturing and rehydration

Yeast is the lowest form of plant life, but it does have at least one useful function—the creation of alcohol. The main objective is to ensure that the brewing wort is colonized quickly by enough strong yeast cells, which drastically reduces the risk of infection. Hence, you need to plan your yeast ahead of brewing to ensure that it gets off to a good start.

A low pitching rate will give a slow fermentation, thus increasing the competition from bacteria and wild yeasts. It will also lead to higher diacetyl levels (diacetyls are a natural by-product of fermentation) and possibly pediococcus infection, the latter of which is, of course, no fun. A high pitching rate will decrease the pH and reduce bacterial growth just as it will the formation of diacetyl. A word here on diacetyl: in strict moderation, diacetyl is not harmful to your beer and its presence is, in fact, relatively acceptable in some beers, particularly more flavorsome ales. This is not a universally shared opinion, however, and some brewers consider it a hindrance to their beer in spite of the occasionally positive flavor it imparts.

Before the yeast cells can go forth and multiply, they will have to be rehydrated to replace the water they lost when they were dried out. As yeasts are living organisms, the rehydration temperature is critical for a good fermenting performance. Your objective here is to reduce the lag phase (the time necessary for the yeasts to start fermenting sugars to alcohol after you have pitched/inoculated the brewing wort). Guaranteed success on this front can be achieved by rehydrating the yeast at a higher temperature than the initial fermentation temperature.

Top-fermenting ale yeasts should be rehydrated at a temperature of 25–29°C (77–84°F) and bottom-fermenting lager yeasts at a temperature range of 21–25°C (70–77°F). For dry yeast like Fermentis, rehydrate by sprinkling the yeast into ten times its own weight of sterile water or wort. Gently stir and leave for 30 minutes, then pitch the resultant cream into the fermentation vessel. Remember to rouse (or stir) first.

THE YEAST BANK

The Brewing Industry Research Center, in Nutfield, Surrey acts as the United Kingdom's yeast bank. Yep, that's right; all commercial brewers deposit strains of their yeast here for safe-keeping and posterity. This is how Westerham Brewery was able to secure the original Black Eagle Brewery yeast that hadn't been used since it closed in 1965.

CULTURE FROM BOTTLE There are a multitude of yeasts available to the homebrewer. If, however, you need one that is commercially unavailable, it's possible to culture a yeast from a bottle-conditioned beer. Unfortunately, the majority of commercial beers are not only filtered but also flash-pasteurized before bottling and so leave little or no yeast trace at all. However, a few brewers will bottle-condition their beers. To be sure if a bottle of beer is suitable, look out for a sediment at the bottom of the bottle when it is held up to the light.

Also bear in mind that commercial brewers will sometimes use two or three different yeasts in a batch of beer. Some of the yeast will be stronger than the others and so you will not necessarily be able to produce the same yeast strain even if you do culture them from the bottle. However, here is how to culture the yeast from a bottle:

1. Thoroughly clean all the equipment during this process. (You'll need to be even more thorough than if you were making a normal batch of beer.)

2. Make a worzt with a specific gravity of 1015–1020.

3. Add a pinch of yeast nutrient to the wort.

4. Provide the yeast with carbohydrates, oxygen, and nutrients, remembering to feed the fragile yeast with only a little wort at a time.

5. Leaving the bottle cap on, wipe over the neck of the bottle and cap with a sanitizing solution, being careful not to disturb the sediment.

6. Pour off the beer and, again, make sure that you don't disturb the sediment.

7. Let the bottle warm up to room temperature, covering the opening with some sanitized aluminum (aluminium) foil.

8. Pour wort down the side of the bottle onto the yeast (using enough to cover the bottom) and swirl it around a little. Replace the aluminum foil.

9. Leave for between 1 to 3 days at a temperature of 70–90°F (21–32°C)—on top of a kitchen cupboard out of direct light will be sufficient.

10. Once signs of fermentation appear (i.e. cloudiness or frothing), transfer the fermenting wort into a small amount of fresh wort (approx. 1 tablespoon).

11. To get enough for a 23-litre-/5-gallon-/6-US-gallon batch, you will need to keep adding the wort in small stages until you have 1.5 litres (51 fl oz). Note that you are feeding the yeast, not drowning it!

Culture from unsettled cask Ideally, take a sample from a fresh unsettled barrel of beer. Make up a couple of pints of DME (dry malt extract), so that when you add a pint of the beer the original gravity is 1040ish. I use a demijohn and mag stirrer, and it can take a few days before results can be seen! Don't use the yeast culture if you don't get enough activity.

Temperature during fermentation

Firstly, always refer to the product packaging or specification sheets. Next, remember that the warmer the temperature at the beginning of the fermentation, the faster the fermentation will start, which will also increase the ester (a flavor compound created during fermentation) and diacetyl levels. So, it is important to regulate top temperatures, but be mindful that for the reabsorption of diacetyl you may have to allow the temperature to rise at the end of fermentation. Diacetyl absorption by the yeast is a good thing (it removes the errant diacetyl from running freely around your beer) and, occasionally, a gentle rise in temperatures can be employed at the end of the fermentation process to achieve good yeast flocculation (removal of sediment from a fluid) and better absorption of diaceytl.

Oxygenating the wort

Aerating your cooled wort immediately before pitching is essential for getting a good start with the fermentation. This can be achieved by rousing (or stirring), aeration, or direct oxygen injection. Whichever method you use, it is crucial that good hygiene is observed at all times. Best

Fermentation Temperature Chart

	Start Temperature	Top Temperature	Diacetyl Rest Temperature	Chill Temperature
Ale	18–20°C (65–68°F)	21–23°C (70–73°F)	Decrease from 20°C (68°F) to 16–17°C (61–63°F) for 24 hours	1–5°C (34–41°F) for chilled and filtered ale 0–12°C (32–54°F) for cask ale
Lager	12°C (54°F)	15°C (60°F)	15°C (60°F) for 24–48 hours	1–3°C (34–37°F)

practice for the homebrewer is to get an aqua pump with micron filters to clean the air passing through. Aerating after pitching should only be performed during the first 12 hours because adding oxygen during late fermentation will increase the aldehyde levels and amplify diacetyl.

A note on beer replicas

Without wanting to demean the efforts of others, who have written extensively on the subject, you simply will not be able to reproduce a beer exactly. You cannot know all the techniques a brewer uses when designing a beer or all the components and variations of his mash. You will also be brewing with vastly different equipment. Many brewers use a different type of yeast for their bottled beer to that of keg or cask—not just to make it harder to obtain, but also to ensure preservation in the bottle.

It is, however, possible to get close and great fun to try. Bear in mind that many beer recipes of the same style often only vary in the grain bill by 56g (2oz) here or there. The grains are predominately the same.

Research is key to creating a reliable copy. Buy a bottle or can and check out the label and the brewers website for hints as to the type of hops and grains used. They will all tell you the ABV (alcohol by volume) and some the OG (original gravity). When you have all this information, compare the color to the EBC chart (see page 29). You can now employ the best cheating service a man has ever selflessly employed for the good of other brewers—Graham Wheeler's excellent "Beer Engine" program for Windows Xp, which is a free download. Simply punch in all your ingredients, the ABV, estimated IBU (International Bittering Units,) and EBC (European Brewing Convention), and the program will work out the weight of grain and hops required. Easy—well, not quite. You will still need to adjust and tweak the recipe once brewed to make it an acceptable copy—add sugars, subtract hops, lighten the grain, add the odd adjunct for head retention; and it may take a few attempts to get it right.

To convert SRM (Standard Research Method) to EBC:

$(SRM \times 2.65) - 1.2 = EBC.$

To convert EBC to SRM:

$(EBC \times 0.375) + 0.46 = SRM.$

Hop Table

Hop Name	AA Range	Substitutions
Admiral (UK)	13.5–16%	Target, Northdown, Challenger
Ahtanum (US)	7–9%	Cascade, Amarillo
Amarillo Gold (US)	6–9%	Cascade, Centennial
Apollo (US)	18–22%	Centennial, Columbus, Amarillo
Blitzen (GR)	11–15%	Horizon, Magnum
Brambling Cross (UK)	5–8%	N/A
Bravo (US)	14–17%	Nugget
Brewer's Gold (UK)	6–8%	N. Brewer, Galena, Eroica,
Bullion (UK)	6–9%	German Chinook, Eroica, Brewer's Gold
Cascade (US)	4.5–7%	Centennial, Amarillo, Columbus
Centennial (US)	9–12%	Galena, Cascade, Columbus
Challenger (UK)	6.5–8.5%	Perle, N. Brewer
Chinook (US)	11–13%	Galena, Columbus, Target
Citra	10–12%	Cascade, Centennial, Ahtanum
Cluster (US)	5.5–8.5%	Eroica, Galena
Columbia (UK)	5.5%	Fuggles, Willamette
Columbus (Tomahawk) (US)	10–16%	Centennial, Nugget, Chinook
Comet (US)	9.5%	N/A
Crystal (US)	2–4.5%	Hersbrucker, Mt. Hood, Liberty
Eroica (US)	9–13%	Galena, N. Brewer, Nugget
First Gold (UK)	6.5–8.5%	ESB EKG, Crystal
Fuggles (UK)	4–5.5%	EKG, US Fuggles, Willamette

Fuggles (US)	4–5.5%	UK Fuggles, Willamette
Galena (US)	10–14%	Eroica, N. Brewer, Cluster, Chinook, Nugget
Glacier (US)	5–9%	Willamette, Fuggles, Goldings,
Goldings, East Kent (EKG)(UK)	4–6%	Fuggles, US Goldings
Goldings (US)	4–6%	EKG, Fuggles, Whitbread, Progress
Green Bullet (NZ)	13.5%	Styrian Goldings
Hallertauer (GR)	3–5%	Crystal, Liberty, Mittelfrueh
Hallertauer (US)	3.5–5.5%	Liberty, Ultra, Hallertauer (GR)
Hallertauer, Hersbrucker (GR)	1.5–5.5%	Mt. Hood, Liberty, Mittelfrueh
Hallertauer, Mittelfrueh (GR)	3–5.5%	Hallertauer, Mt. Hood, Liberty,
Hallertauer (NZ)	8.5%	Hallertauer, Mittelfrueh
Herald (UK)	12%	High-alpha English hops
Horizon (US)	11–14%	Magnum
Independent (US)	6%	Lagers N/A
Liberty (US)	3–6%	Mittlefrueh, Mt. Hood, Crystal
Lublin (Poland)	3–5%	Saaz, Tettnanger
Magnum (GR)	13–15%	Horizon
Magnum (US)	13–15%	Willamette, Fuggles, EKG.
Mt. Hood (US)	3–8%	Hersbrucker, Liberty, Crystal
Mt. Rainier (US)	6–8%	Hallertauer, Fuggles
Nelson Sauvin (NZ)	11–13%	N/A
Newport (US)	11.5–17%	Galena, Nugget, Fuggles, Magnum, Brewer's Gold

Hop Name	AA Range	Substitutions
Northdown (UK)	7.5–9.5%	N. Brewer
Northern Brewer (GR)	8–10%	Hallertauer, Mittelfrueh, Nugget
Nugget (US)	9–13%	Columbus, Target, Galena
Orion (GR)	7–9%	Perle
Pacific Gem (NZ)	15%	Bullion
Palisade (US)	5.5–9.5%	Willamette, Goldings
Perle (GR)	5–9%	Chinook, Galena, N. Brewer
Phoenix (UK)	4–8%	Challenger, EKG, Northdown
Pilgrim (UK)	11–13%	N/A
Pioneer (UK)	8–10%	EKG
Pride of Ringwood (AUS)	7–10%	Cluster, Galena
Primiant (Czech)	7–9%	N/A
Progress (UK)	6–8%	Fuggles, EKG
Revolution (US)	5%	N/A
Riwaka (NZ)	5–7%	Cascade, Centennial
Saaz (Czech)	3–4.5%	Tettnanger, Lublin, US Saaz
Saaz (US)	3–5%	Czech Saaz, Tettnanger
Santiam (US)	5–8%	Tettnanger, Spalt, Select Spalt
Saphir (GR)	4%	N/A
Select Spalt (GR)	4–6%	Spalt, Saaz, Tettnanger
Simcoe (US)	12–14%	N/A

Slovenian Celeia (Slovenia)	3–6%	Saaz, Styrian Goldings
Sorachi Ace (Japan)	13–16%	N/A
Southern Cross (NZ)	13%	N/A
Sovereign (UK)	4–6%	N/A
Spalt (GR)	4–6%	Saaz, Tettnanger, Select Spalt
Sterling (US)	6–9%	Saaz, Lublin
Sticklebract (NZ)	13–15%	N. Brewer
Strisselspalt (FR)	2–4%	Mt. Hood Crystal, Hersbrucker
Styrian Aurora (Slovenia)	7–9%	N. Brewer, Styrian Goldings
Styrian Goldings (Slovenia)	4–6%	Fuggles, Willamette
Summit (US)	17–19%	Simcoe, Amarillo
Sun (US)	14%	High-alpha US hops
Super Alpha (NZ)	13%	N/A
Target (UK)	9.5–12.5%	EKG, Fuggles, Willamette
Tettnang (GR)	3.5–5.5%	Saaz, Spalt, Tettnanger
Tradition (GR)	5–7%	Mittelfrueh, Liberty, Ultra
Ultra (US)	2–4%	Liberty, Hallertauer, Saaz
Vanguard (US)	5–7%	Hallertauer Mittelfrueh, Saaz
Warrior (US)	14–17%	Nugget
Whitbread Golding Variety (UK)	5–7%	EKG, Progress
Willamette (US)	4–6%	Fuggles, EKG, Tett., Sty., Goldings
Yakima Golding (US)	5%	EKG, Progress, Fuggles
Zeus (US)	13–17%	Other high alpha hops

Troubleshooting for Beerheads

Why is my beer flat?

Carbonating beer naturally with an active yeast can be tricky and it may take a couple of attempts to get a foamy head to your liking. If the beer is flat, then try using a couple more grams of bottling sugar or add 28g (1oz) of flaked wheat to the mash.

Why is my beer thin and watery?

This shows that not enough proteins were produced from the mash (proteins give the beer body). Try using 28–56g (1–2oz) of protein-rich wheat, and then mash hotter and shorter to achieve a much richer wort.

Why has my beer become thick and jelly-like?

Chuck it! This beer has a major infection. Acetobater and Pediococcus bacteria are present and have produced a polysaccharide goo. Reread the sanitizing section and sanitize better.

Is my beer safe to drink if it smells of old socks/cheese?

I wouldn't drink this beer if you offered it to me. Although it won't do you any harm, it is not going to taste good. This has happened because stale hops were used. Hops should smell sharp and fresh, not stale or musty. The solution is to store your hops in air-tight containers or even freeze any leftover hops for the next brew.

Why does my beer look hazy?

This will not spoil the taste, but, aesthetically, it isn't pleasing after all that hard work. The reason the beer is hazy is that the proteins did not settle out and re-suspended during the chilling process. This also may have happened because of over-priming the bottles. Another reason is that the malt used may have been moldy. So, make sure your sanitizing is really top-notch, ensure the malt is within date and not moldy, and also check you are not over-priming the bottles.

Why does my beer smell like rotten eggs?
This could be one of two things: infection or the brew is just too long (especially if it is a lager). To solve this, leave the brew (if lager) for another week and see if the smell dissipates. If it doesn't, then it's an infection and is down to poor sanitizing. Obviously, throw any infected brew down the drain.

Why does my beer smell like a barnyard?
The hop molecules have been hit by certain light waves, which have broken them apart. Then, the pieces have combined with hydrogen sulphide to produce the awful smell. Beer must be bottled in brown glass and stored out of direct light.

Why does my beer froth over when I open the bottle?
This is a classic sign that your brew has been infected with a wild yeast. However, if none of the normal sourness associated with wild yeast is present, then you could have simply over-primed the bottles. Take extra care over your sanitizing techniques or, if the latter is suspected, just tone down the level of priming sugar used. I would also suggest checking your malt is not moldy.

ENJOY!
If you are bored with the beers available commercially, then homebrewing is an option. Don't be put off if you are unsuccessful on your first attempt. Remember, practice really will make perfect and it happens to us all. In homebrewing circles, you are in good company, so let's get to work!

THE RECIPES

PATER'S BEER

This is a type of Trappist beer, which, as the name suggests, originated from a Cistercian monastery in La Trappe, in Soligny, France. Although the Trappist monks were sworn to a life of strict asceticism, they were eventually allowed to brew beer. Paters beer or "father's beer" is a Trappist beer variety that was initially only meant for the monks themselves to drink. All Trappist beers are ales that are top-fermented and bottle-conditioned.

Original gravity	1085	
Water	23 litres/5 gallons/6 US gallons	
Mash Roll	Weight	
Pale malt	3.85kg (8½lb)	
Munich malt	453g (1lb)	
Crystal malt	226g (8oz)	
Black malt	28g (1oz)	
Mash Schedule	1 hour	
In the Boil	Weight	Time
Dark brown sugar	453g (1lb)	90 minutes
Hallertauer	56g (2oz)	60 minutes from end
UK Goldings	28g (1oz)	60 minutes from end
Protofloc	1 teaspoon	15 minutes from end
Honey	226g (8oz)	at the end of the boil
Boil duration	1½ hours	
Yeast	Trappist ale yeast—WLP-500	
Target FG	1018	
Target ABV	8%	

ABBEY BEER

As the name indicates, Abbey Beer is a monastic style of beer. In this recipe, I have developed my own version of an abbey beer for you to sample. There are in total 18 certified commercial producers of this style of beer in existence today; that is to say, this is not a rigid style of brewing. However, you will usually find that most monastic-style beers are distinctive and made to an exceptionally high standard.

Original gravity	1062
Water	23 litres/5 gallons/6 US gallons

Mash Roll	Weight
Pilsner malt	4.8kg (10½lb)
Munich malt	453g (1lb)
Chocolate malt	28g (1oz)

Mash Schedule	1 hour

In the Boil	Weight	Time
Willamette	28g (1oz)	60 minutes
Fuggles	28g (1oz)	15 minutes from end
Protofloc	1 teaspoon	15 minutes from end

Boil duration	1 hour
Yeast	Belgian Abbey—WY-1214
Target FG	1008
Target ABV	4.6%

A WORD TO THE WISE

For most recipes in this book, no starter yeast is required. You simply need to use Wyeast labs smack-packs.

AMBER ALE

Amber in name, amber in color. This is a great beer to serve with pasta covered in shavings of Parmesan cheese.

Original gravity	1080	
Water	23 litres/5 gallons/6 US gallons	
Mash Roll	Weight	
Dark Munich malt	5.4kg (12lb)	
Dextrose (corn sugar)	970g (2lb)	
Mash Schedule	1 hour	
In the Boil	Weight	Time
Northern Brewer	28g (1oz)	60 minutes
Protofloc	1 teaspoon	15 minutes from end
Boil duration	1 hour	
Yeast	Belgian—WY-3522	
Target FG	1020	
Target ABV	5.3%	

A WORD TO THE WISE

Every monastery used to brew its own beer for the monks and also for visitors. Today, only a few monasteries still brew beer, although commercial brewers make beers with monastic connections.

BLONDE ALE

This ale has a fantastic, deep golden color that sets off the creamy white head to great effect.

Original gravity	1050	
Water	23 litres/5 gallons/6 US gallons	
Mash Roll	Weight	
Pale malt	4.3kg (9½lb)	
Light crystal malt	453g (1lb)	
Carapils	113g (4oz)	
Caramalt	113g (4oz)	
Mash Schedule	1 hour	
In the Boil	Weight	Time
Perle	31g (1oz)	60 minutes
Cascade	28g (1oz)	10 minutes from end
Protofloc	1 teaspoon	15 minutes from end
Boil duration	1 hour	
Yeast	American ale—WY-1056	
Target FG	1012	
Target ABV	4.9%	

A WORD TO THE WISE

In Blonde Ale, depending on the hops used, you are aiming for an earthy hop nose with a lightly sweet Pils malt character.

ELDERFLOWER BLOND

With its high hopping rate and the elderflowers, this is a refreshing, aromatic summer ale.

Original gravity	1073
Water	23 litres/5 gallons/6 US gallons

Mash Roll	Weight
2-row pale malt	4.3kg (9½lb)
Munich malt	453g (1lb)
Carapils	453g (1lb)
Torrified wheat	226g (8oz)

Mash Schedule	1 hour

In the Boil	Weight	Time
Hallertauer	35g (1¼oz)	60 minutes
Saaz	28g (1oz)	10 minutes from end
Fresh or dried elderflowers	200g (7oz)	at flame-out
Protofloc	1 teaspoon	15 minutes from end

Boil duration	1 hour
Yeast	Belgian Ardennes—WY-3522
Target FG	1010
Target ABV	5.5%

"Always do sober what you said you'd do drunk. That will teach you to keep your mouth shut."

ERNEST HEMINGWAY (1899-1961)

GOLDEN ALE

A fine example of a Belgian classic, the honey used in this recipe really shines through.

Original gravity	1073	
Water	23 litres/5 gallons/6 US gallons	
Mash Roll	Weight	
Pilsner malt	4.9kg (11lb)	
Dextrose (corn sugar)	907g (2lb)	
Torrified wheat	226g (8oz)	
Honey	226g (8oz)	
Mash Schedule	1 hour	
In the Boil	Weight	Time
Hallertauer	15g (½oz)	60 minutes
Styrian Goldings	31g (1oz)	60 minutes
Hallertauer	15g (½oz)	30 minutes from end
Saaz	15g (½oz)	30 minutes from end
Styrian Goldings	31g (1oz)	30 minutes from end
Saaz	15g (½oz)	1 minute from end
Protofloc	1 teaspoon	15 minutes from end
Boil duration	1 hour	
Yeast	Belgian Ardennes—WY-3522	
Target FG	1010	
Target ABV	8.4%	

A WORD TO THE WISE

The use of the Nelson Sauvin hop is optional, but does add a special edge to this brew.

CHAMPAGNE BEER

This is essentially a beer that is brewed in the normal way, but then fermented with Champagne yeast. The original Champagne beer would have been trippel-matured with Champagne yeast and then aged in Champagne caves with the bottles at an angle so that the yeast could collect in the necks before being frozen and removed. This beer makes a great aperitif and can easily become a favorite among those who do not really like beer.

Original gravity	1082	
Water	23 litres/5 gallons/6 US gallons	
Mash Roll	Weight	
Pilsner malt	3.35kg (7¼lb)	
2-row pale malt	1.7kg (3¾lb)	
Carapils	335g (11¾oz)	
Rye malt	335g (11¾oz)	
Belgian light candi sugar	1kg (2¼lb)	
Mash Schedule	1 hour	
In the Boil	Weight	Time
Fuggles	38g (1¼lb)	60 minutes
Hellertauer	21g (¾oz)	60 minutes
Nelson Sauvin	10g (¼oz)	5 minutes from end
Saaz	19g (¾oz)	1 minute from end
Protofloc	1 teaspoon	15 minutes from end
Boil duration	1 hour	
Yeast	Pasteur Champagne—WY-4021	
Target FG	1016	
Target ABV	4.7%	

DUBBEL

Belgian brewers are renowned for their ability to create great beers. Considering the complexity of the flavors in Belgian beer, you would be forgiven for thinking they were alchemists but, traditionally, these brews were created in monasteries because the monks were able to obtain ingredients from around the world.

Original gravity	1060	
Water	23 litres/5 gallons/6 US gallons	
Mash Roll	Weight	
Belgian Pilsener malt	4.9kg (11lb)	
Belgian biscuit malt	341g (12oz)	
Belgian aromatic malt	264g (9¼oz)	
Caramunich	34g (1¼oz)	
Belgian special B	11g (¼oz)	
Mash Schedule	1 hour	
In the Boil	Weight	Time
Belgian candi sugar amber	600g (1¼lb)	90 minutes
Styrian Aurora	24g (¾oz)	60 minutes from end
Czech Saaz	10g (¼oz)	15 minutes from end
Protofloc	1 teaspoon	15 minutes from end
Boil duration	1½ hours	
Yeast	Belgian Abbey—WY-1214	
Target FG	1010	
Target ABV	6.6%	

A WORD TO THE WISE

The hops in Trippel Beer are there, ultimately, to balance the sweetness of the malts.

TRIPPEL

The hops in this beer create a spicy, clove-like aroma with a rounded malt flavor, masking the high alcohol content.

Original gravity	1082
Water	23 litres/5 gallons/6 US gallons

Mash Roll	Weight
Pilsner malt	3.35kg (7¼lb)
2-row pale malt	1.7kg (3¾lb)
Carapils	335g (11¾oz)
Rye malt	335g (11¾oz)
Belgian light candi sugar	1kg (2¼lb)

Mash Schedule	1 hour

In the Boil	Weight	Time
UK Goldings	38g (1¼oz)	60 minutes
Hellertauer	21g (¾oz)	60 minutes
Saaz	19g (¾oz)	1 minute from end
Protofloc	1 teaspoon	15 minutes from end

Boil duration	1 hour
Yeast	Belgian Abbey—WY-1214
Expected FG	1016
Expected ABV	7.5%

QUADDRUPPEL

This style of beer is the strongest, richest, and most complex in flavor of all the Belgian beers.

Original gravity	1084
Water	23 litres/5 gallons/6 US gallons

Mash Roll	Weight
Maris otter	6.3kg (13¾lb)
Dark Munich malt	453g (1lb)
Belgian dark candi sugar	453g (1lb)
Dark brown sugar	340g (12oz)
Light brown sugar	340g (12oz)
Caramunich III	113g (4oz)
Belgian special B	28g (1oz)

Mash Schedule	1½ hours

In the Boil	Weight	Time
Saaz	28g (1oz)	60 minutes
Perle	28g (1oz)	15 minutes from end
Peppercorns (crushed)	1 teaspoon	20 minutes from end
Protofloc	1 teaspoon	15 minutes from end

Boil duration	1 hour
Yeast	Belgian Abbey ale—WY-1762
Target FG	1015
Target ABV	9.2%

RED BEER

Strong on taste and alcohol, red beer contains a little chocolate malt, giving it a smoky flavor.

Original gravity	1064	
Water	23 litres/5 gallons/6 US gallons	
Mash Roll	Weight	
Maris otter	4.9kg (11lb)	
Caramunich	226g (8oz)	
Aromatic malt	110g (3¾oz)	
Chocolate malt	28g (1oz)	
Mash Schedule	1 hour	
In the Boil	Weight	Time
Tettnanger	35g (1¼oz)	60 minutes
Galena	14g (½oz)	15 minutes from end
Styrian Goldings	7g (¼oz)	15 minutes from end
Candi sugar	453g (1lb)	near the end
(light to medium in color)		
Protofloc	1 teaspoon	15 minutes from end
Boil duration	1 hour	
Yeast	Belgian ale—WY-1762	
Target FG	1015	
Target ABV	8%	

FLEMISH RED

Traditionally matured in oak casks, the roasted malts give this beer its distinctive, deep reddish brown hue.

Original gravity	1052	
Water	23 litres/5 gallons/6 US gallons	
Mash Roll	**Weight**	
Vienna malt	3.6kg (8lb)	
Flaked maize	1.3kg (2¾lb)	
Caravienne	453g (1lb)	
Caramel Pilsner malt	453g (1lb)	
Belgian aromatic malt	453g (1lb)	
Belgian special B	85g (3oz)	
Mash Schedule	1 hour	
In the Boil	**Weight**	**Time**
Fuggles	28g (1oz)	75 minutes
UK Goldings	14g (½oz)	15 minutes from end
Protofloc	1 teaspoon	15 minutes from end
Boil duration	1¼ hours	
Yeast	Belgian ale—WY-1762	
Target FG	1012	
Target ABV	5.3%	

"Always do
sober what
you said
you'd do
drunk. That
will teach
you to keep
your mouth
shut."

ERNEST
HEMINGWAY
(1899-1961)

A WORD TO THE WISE

Try adding some cardamom pods to your Saison Beer during the boil.

SAISON

This beer is a Flemish classic and its name simply means "season." Once brewed as a refreshment for Belgian farm workers as they gathered in the harvest in late summer, this brew originates from the Walloon, a French-speaking region of Belgium.

Original gravity	1049	
Water	23 litres/5 gallons/6 US gallons	
Mash Roll	**Weight**	
Pilsner malt	3kg (6½lb)	
Vienna malt	1.1kg (2½lb)	
Torrified wheat	240g (8½oz)	
Medium crystal malt	210g (7¼oz)	
Belgian aromatic malt	160g (5½oz)	
Mash Schedule	1 hour	
In the Boil	**Weight**	**Time**
German Brewers Gold	19g (¾oz)	90 minutes
UK Goldings	10g (¼oz)	30 minutes from end
Slovenian Styrian Goldings	12g (½oz)	10 minutes from end
Star anise	10g (¼oz)	20 minutes from end
Lemon zest	1 whole	10 minutes from end
Orange zest	2 whole	10 minutes from end
Coriander seeds (crushed)	20g (¾oz)	10 minutes from end
Freshly ground black pepper	1 teaspoon	5 minutes from end
Protofloc	1 teaspoon	15 minutes from end
Boil duration	1½ hours	
Yeast	Belgian Saison—WY-3724	
Target FG	1009	
Target ABV	5.3%	

CHRISTMAS BEER

This is a specialty beer that is very strong, as well as full of spice and robust flavors. Every brewery will have its own take on a Christmas beer and you should be prepared to experiment with your own quantities of spices to achieve just the right taste for you. The recipe given here is meant to provide you with a guideline only, so be brave and try your hand at making something of your very own that's full of Christmas cheer.

A WORD TO THE WISE

For a delicious Christmas beer, try just adding 3 cinnamon sticks and 6 whole cloves with the hops and then boil as normal.

Original gravity	1058	
Water	23 litres/5 gallons/6 US gallons	

Mash Roll	Weight	
American 2-row pale malt	4kg (8¾lb)	
Vienna malt	1.1kg (2½lb)	
Caramel malt	453g (1lb)	
Victory malt	453g (1lb)	
Caramunich	226g (8oz)	
Belgian dark candi sugar	226g (8oz)	
Honey malt	226g (8oz)	
Carafa I	113g (4oz)	

Mash Schedule	1 hour	

In the Boil	Weight	Time
Saaz	16g (½oz)	60 minutes
Hersbrucker	16g (½oz)	60 minutes
Styrian Goldings	14g (½oz)	60 minutes
Styrian Goldings	14g (½oz)	15 minutes from end
Hersbrucker	15g (½oz)	5 minutes from end
Star anise	10g (¼oz)	20 minutes from end
Cinnamon sticks	3	10 minutes from end
Whole cloves	7	10 minutes from end
Fresh root ginger (chopped)	30g (1oz)	10 minutes from end
Ground nutmeg	1 teaspoon	10 minutes from end
Protofloc	1 teaspoon	15 minutes from end

Boil duration	1 hour	
Yeast	Belgian ale—WY-1762	
Target FG	1015	
Target ABV	7.3%	

WHEAT BEER

A traditional Flemish beer that does not depend solely on the hops to add flavor to the malt.

Original gravity	1046	
Water	23 litres/5 gallons/6 US gallons	
Mash Roll	Weight	
Torrified wheat	2.48kg (5½lb)	
Pilsner malt	2.48kg (5½lb)	
Mash Schedule	1 hour	
In the Boil	Weight	Time
Fuggles	31g (1oz)	90 minutes
Orange zest (without pith)	15g (½oz)	15 minutes from end
Coriander seeds (crushed)	23g (¾oz)	10 minutes from end
Cumin seeds	5g (1/8oz)	10 minutes from end
Protofloc	1 teaspoon	15 minutes from end
Boil duration	1½ hours	
Yeast	Belgian wheat—WY-3942	
Expected FG	1011	
Expected ABV	4.6%	

SPICED ALE

A perfect beer for Christmas. You can add other spices such as a pinch of cinnamon to increase its complexity.

Original gravity	1048	
Water	23 litres/5 gallons/6 US gallons	

Mash Roll	Weight	
English 2-row pale malt	4kg (8¾lb)	
Medium crystal malt	210g (7¼oz)	
Honey	600g (1¼lb)	

Mash Schedule	1½ hours	

In the Boil	Weight	Time
Target	30g (1oz)	90 minutes
Hallertau Hersbruck	35g (1¼oz)	10 minutes from end
Orange zest	35g (1¼oz)	15 minutes from end
Fresh root ginger (chopped)	25g (⅞oz)	15 minutes from end
Protofloc	1 teaspoon	15 minutes from end

Boil duration	1½ hours
Yeast	Saison—WY-3711
Target FG	1010
Target ABV	4.8%

BLACKBERRY WITBIER

A beer with a subtle sweetness, the off-white head you get on pouring quickly disappears.

Original gravity	1040	
Water	23 litres/5 gallons/6 US gallons	

Mash Roll	Weight	
2-row pale malt	2.2kg (4¾lb)	
White wheat malt	2.2kg (4¾lb)	
Flaked oats	570g (1¼lb)	
Munich malt	113g (4oz)	

Mash Schedule	1½ hours	

In the Boil	Weight	Time
Goldings	28g (1oz)	60 minutes
Goldings	14g (½oz)	20 minutes from end
Protofloc	1 teaspoon	15 minutes from end
Blackberries	1.4kg (3lb)	at primary fermentation for 3 days

Boil duration	1 hour	
Yeast	Belgian Witbier—WY-3944	
Target FG	1015	
Target ABV	6.1%	

"Drunk words are sober thoughts."

ANONYMOUS

A WORD TO THE WISE

When using citrus fruits, use the peel and juice from the fruit, taking care not to introduce any of the pith because this will impart a bitter taste.

WILDFLOWER WITBIER

When poured, this beer should have a well-rounded, golden color and a light sweet aroma.

Original gravity	1052	
Water	23 litres/5 gallons/6 US gallons	
Mash Roll	Weight	
White wheat	2.23kg (5lb)	
2-row pale malt	1.8kg (4lb)	
Vienna malt	412g (14½oz)	
Flaked barley	110g (3¾oz)	
Mash Schedule	1 hour	
In the Boil	Weight	Time
Cascade	16g (½oz)	60 minutes
Cascade	16g (½oz)	10 minutes from end
Oranges	6	20 minutes from end
Grapefruit	1	20 minutes from end
Chamomile teabag	1	15 minutes from end
Coriander seeds (crushed)	1 teaspoon	10 minutes from end
Protofloc	1 teaspoon	15 minutes from end
Boil duration	1 hour	
Yeast	Belgian Witbier—WY-3944	
Target FG	1009	
Target ABV	5.2%	

STOUT

Belgian Stout was first made by a small number of artisan brewers, but caught on in America where great stouts have been made.

Original gravity	1080	
Water	23 litres/5 gallons/6 US gallons	
Mash Roll	Weight	
Pilsen malt	5.4kg (12lb)	
Munich malt	910g (2lb)	
Torrified wheat	453g (1lb)	
Chocolate malt	453g (1lb)	
Roast barley	453g (1lb)	
Belgian special B	453g (1lb)	
Mash Schedule	1 hour	
In the Boil	Weight	Time
Belgian dark candi syrup	453g (1lb)	90 minutes
Northern Brewer	28g (1oz)	60 minutes from end
Fuggles	28g (1oz)	30 minutes from end
Fuggles	12g (½oz)	at the end
Protofloc	1 teaspoon	15 minutes from end
Boil duration	1½ hours	
Yeast	Belgian Abbey II—WY-1762	
Target FG	1010	
Target ABV	7.5%	

A WORD TO THE WISE

For stout, boil down the first runnings in order to caramelize.

TAFELBIER

Literally meaning "table beer," weak Tafelbier was often found in Belgian school refectories up until the 1970s.

Original gravity	1023	
Water	23 litres/5 gallons/6 US gallons	
Mash Roll	Weight	
Maris otter	1kg (2¼lb)	
Caravienne	453g (1lb)	
Torrified wheat	226g (8oz)	
Belgian aromatic malt	170g (6oz)	
Belgian light candi sugar	141g (5oz)	
Mash Schedule	1 hour	
In the Boil	Weight	Time
Tradition	10g (¼oz)	60 minutes
Protofloc	1 teaspoon	15 minutes from end
Boil duration	1 hour	
Yeast	Belgian ale—WY-1762	
Target FG	1004	
Target ABV	2.5%	

Chapter 2

BRITISH BEERS

A WORD TO THE WISE

For Bitter, try using Northern Brewer instead of Northdown as a hop variation.

BITTER

This is the English term for pale ale. There are five variations in strength of bitter. It is most commonly sold as an ordinary Bitter (usually described as an IPA), which generally has an ABV of around 4.1%. Traditionally, IPAs were around 7%, but the style has been watered down by big breweries in the UK. Please note, modern US IPAs have the higher ABV of the originals. Best Bitter has an ABV of 4.2–4.7%, while the remaining three variations, referred to as Special Bitter, Extra Special Bitter, and Premium Bitter, have varying ABV percentages.

Original gravity	1037	
Water	23 litres/5 gallons/6 US gallons	
Mash Roll	Weight	
Pale ale malt	3.65kg (8lb)	
Torrified wheat	265g (9¼oz)	
Medium crystal malt	100g (3½oz)	
Black malt	65g (2¼oz)	
Mash Schedule	1 hour	
In the Boil	Weight	Time
UK Northdown	20g (¾oz)	90 minutes
UK First Gold	10g (¼oz)	45 minutes from end
UK Bramling Cross	10g (¼oz)	10 minutes from end
Irish moss	1 teaspoon	15 minutes from end
Boil duration	1½ hours	
Yeast	Safale–DCL–S04	
Target FG	1009	
Target ABV	3.9%	

BEST BITTER

Once the preferred choice of the working man, Best Bitter is a good starting-point for any aspiring homebrewer.

Original gravity	1047	
Water	23 litres/5 gallons/6 US gallons	
Mash Roll	Weight	
Pale ale malt	4.9kg (10¾lb)	
Crystal malt	200g (7oz)	
Chocolate malt	45g (1½oz)	
Mash Schedule	1 hour	
In the Boil	Weight	Time
UK Challenger	22g (¾oz)	90 minutes
UK Bramling Cross	20g (¾oz)	20 minutes from end
UK Fuggles	16g (½oz)	5 minutes from end
Protofloc/Irish moss	1 teaspoon	15 minutes from end
Boil duration	1½ hours	
Yeast	London ale—WY-1318	
Target FG	1012	
Target ABV	4.6%	

PALE ALE

Pale Ale used to be brewed using a malt dried with coke. It is a great base for experimenting with different hops.

Original gravity	1049	
Water	23 litres/5 gallons/6 US gallons	
Mash Roll	**Weight**	
Pale malt	3.6kg (8lb)	
Carapils	226g (8oz)	
Caramunich	226g (8oz)	
Mash Schedule		
In the Boil	**Weight**	**Time**
Northern Brewer	31g (1oz)	60 minutes
Fuggles	17g (½oz)	15 minutes from end
Goldings	11g (¼oz)	10 minutes from end
Protofloc	1 teaspoon	15 minutes from end
Boil duration	1 hour	
Yeast	British ale II—WY-1335	
Target FG	1013	
Target ABV	4.6%	

EXTRA SPECIAL BITTER

An Extra Special Bitter usually uses British hops and has lots of malty, fruity flavor.

Original gravity	1053	
Water	23 litres/5 gallons/6 US gallons	
Mash Roll	Weight	
Pale ale malt	4.93kg (10¾lb)	
Medium crystal malt	290g (10¼oz)	
Torrified wheat	210g (7¼oz)	
Chocolate malt	115g (4oz)	
Mash Schedule	1 hour	
In the Boil	Weight	Time
Light brown sugar	115g (4oz)	90 minutes
Williamette	19g (¾oz)	90 minutes
UK Bramling Cross	18g (½oz)	30 minutes from end
UK Goldings	13g (½oz)	30 minutes from end
UK Goldings	14g (½oz)	10 minutes from end
Protofloc	1 teaspoon	15 minutes from end
Boil duration	1½ hours	
Yeast	British ale II—WY-1335	
Target FG	1013	
Target ABV	5.3%	

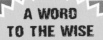

A WORD TO THE WISE

Extra Special Bitter is
a little more bitter than
its standard bitter
counterparts and has
a higher alcohol content.
It is really more
of a slow-and-savor
kind of brew!

A WORD
TO THE WISE

IPA has quite a long
maturing time due
to the large amount
of hops that go
into it.

INDIA PALE ALE

A rather enterprising brewer from England decided during the British occupation of India to develop a beer that could mature on the boat journey rather than in a cellar back in England, thus making good use of the empty cargo ships on their return trip to India. This beer, known as IPA, became incredibly popular with the expats, which is easy to understand given its fantastic hoppy flavor and middling strength.

Original gravity	1052	
Water	23 litres/5 gallons/6 US gallons	
Mash Roll Pale ale malt Medium crystal malt	Weight 5.25kg (11½lb) 420g (14¾oz)	
Mash Schedule	1 hour	
In the Boil Challenger UK First Gold Protofloc	Weight 30g (1oz) 13g (½oz) 1 teaspoon	Time 90 minutes 10 minutes from end 15 minutes from end
Boil duration	1½ hours	
Yeast	Safale—DCL-S04	
Target FG	1041	
Target ABV	5%	

LIGHT SPRING ALE

Although lightly colored and refreshing, this ale is still quite heavy with a high ABV for the style.

Original gravity	1049	
Water	23 litres/5 gallons/6 US gallons	
Mash Roll	Weight	
Pale malt	3.6kg (8lb)	
Aromatic malt	226g (8oz)	
Caravienne	226g (8oz)	
Carafa I	58g (2oz)	
Mash Schedule	1½ hours	
In the Boil	Weight	Time
Goldings	28g (1oz)	80 minutes
Goldings	14g (½oz)	20 minutes from end
Goldings	14g (½oz)	10 minutes from end
Protofloc	1 teaspoon	15 minutes from end
Boil duration	1 hour 20 minutes	
Yeast	British ale II—WY-1335	
Target FG	1013	
Target ABV	4.6%	

GOLDEN SUMMER BEER

When poured into the glass, Golden Summer Beer has a hazy golden color that makes it perfect for drinking on a hot summer's day. It has a full-on, tea-and-hop aroma. Summer beer may be thin, but it is blessed with a lasting head and a delicious taste of wheat and lemon. These summery flavors are gently offset by the subtle spiciness of the coriander seeds which are added at the end of the boil.

Original gravity	1045	
Water	23 litres/5 gallons/6 US gallons	
Mash Roll Maris otter	Weight 4.5kg (10lb)	
Mash Schedule	1 hour	
In the Boil	Weight	Time
Hallertauer	15g (½oz)	60 minutes
Crystal	15g (½oz)	30 minutes from end
Saaz	15g (½oz)	30 minutes from end
Crystal	31g (1oz)	15 minutes from end
Coriander seeds (crushed)	1 tablespoon	30 minutes from end
Protofloc	1 teaspoon	15 minutes from end
Boil duration	1 hour	
Yeast	Belgian Ardennes—WY-3522	
Target FG	1010	
Target ABV	4.5%	

OLD ALE

Traditionally, the name "old ale" was used to describe ales kept over by a brewery and sold at a premium. Sometimes, stock (or very old) ale was blended with a younger ale to tone down the acidity and create an old ale.

Original gravity	1071
Water	23 litres/5 gallons/6 US gallons

Mash Roll	Weight	
Pale ale malt	6.58kg (14½lb)	
Medium crystal malt	730g (1½lb)	

Mash Schedule	1½ hours	

In the Boil	Weight	Time
UK Fuggles	105g (3¾oz)	90 minutes
UK Goldings	25g (¾oz)	15 minutes from end
Protofloc	1 teaspoon	15 minutes from end

Boil duration	1½ hours
Yeast	London ale—WY-1028
Target	FG1017
Target ABV	7.2%

SCOTCH ALE

"Wee Heavy," this sweet, full-bodied ale has a low hop content and tastes of toffee and caramel. Thick and malty, Scotch Ale uses specialty malts to bring out its full character.

Original gravity	1070
Water	23 litres/5 gallons/6 US gallons

Mash Roll	Weight
Pale ale malt	3.4kg (7½lb)
Amber malt	450g (1lb)
Dark crystal malt	172g (6oz)
Roasted barley	27g (1oz)

Mash Schedule	1 hour	

In the Boil	Weight	Time
UK Goldings	28g (1oz)	90 minutes

Boil duration	1½ hours
Yeast	Scottish ale—WY-1728
Target FG	1020
Target ABV	7.5%

A WORD TO THE WISE

Although I have used UK Goldings, throw in any old hops that you have left over as they are only needed for bittering. Use a pinch of peated malt for an added smoky flavor.

BROWN ALE

Brown Ale first appeared in Northern England. The ale was commonly bought straight from the brewery. For this reason, it is sometimes known as a "running beer." With a great caramelized hue, brown ale is lighter but stronger than a mild ale.

Original gravity	1041	
Water	23 litres/5 gallons/6 US gallons	
Mash Roll	Weight	
Pale ale malt	2.38kg (5¼lb)	
Caramel malt	907g (2lb)	
Chocolate malt	113g (4oz)	
Mash Schedule	1 hour	
In the Boil	Weight	Time
UK Fuggles	28g (1oz)	90 minutes
UK Goldings	28g (1oz)	15 minutes from end
Light brown sugar	453g (1lb)	90 minutes
Boil duration	1½ hours	
Yeast	British ale II—WY-1335	
Target FG	1013	
Target ABV	4.32%	

"No soldier can fight unless he is properly fed on beef and beer."

JOHN CHURCHILL,
FIRST DUKE OF MARLBOROUGH (1650-1722)

A WORD
TO THE WISE

In Brown Ale, the use of
English ale yeast will
achieve a sweeter finish.
If you prefer to have a
mid-range outcome, then
try using a London ale
yeast instead.

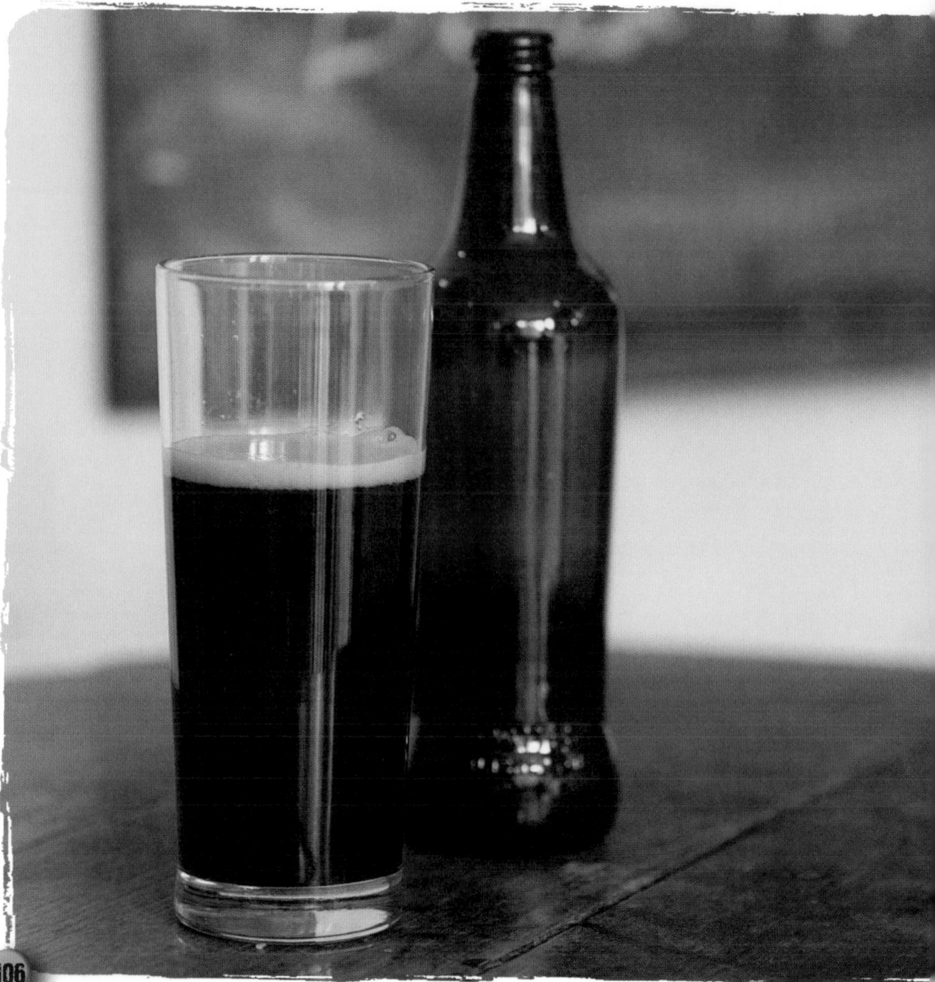

MILD

Although not highly hopped, Mild can actually be a tasty brew, especially if you enjoy malt flavors. Milds originated in 17th-century England when hops were introduced from France, Germany, and Holland. English brewers could then reduce the gravity of strong ales, using the hops for their preserving qualities, and thus produce a good all-round rew. Mild is a nice recipe for the homebrewer, although the challenge is to get big flavor into this style of brewing.

Original gravity	1032	
Water	23 litres/5 gallons/6 US gallons	
Mash Roll	Weight	
Pale ale malt	3.1kg (6¾lb)	
Medium crystal malt	215g (7½oz)	
Chocolate malt	110g (3¾oz)	
Torrified Wheat	100g (3½oz)	
Mash Schedule	1 hour	
In the Boil	Weight	Time
UK Challenger	18g (½oz)	90 minutes
UK Fuggle	10g (¼oz)	90 minutes
UK Goldings	10g (¼oz)	10 minutes from end
Protofloc	1 teaspoon	15 minutes from end
Boil duration	1½ hours	
Yeast	London ale—WY-1028	
Target FG	1009	
Target ABV	3.1%	

DARK RUBY MILD

A great mild ale, Dark Ruby Mild has a sweet malty base and a slight hop balance. When you pour this ale into your glass, it should have a gorgeous, ruby-red color as well as a creamy colored, almost tan, head. This is very much an easy-drinking beer in spite of the higher ABV. Warming and delicious, it is just the tipple to imbibe sitting in front of a roaring fire on a cold winter's evening.

Original gravity	1060	
Water	23 litres/5 gallons/6 US gallons	
Mash Roll	Weight	
Maris otter	5kg (11lb)	
Chocolate malt	113g (4oz)	
Medium crystal malt	1.5g (1/32oz)	
Mash Schedule	1 hour	
In the Boil	Weight	Time
Williamette	41g (1½oz)	90 minutes
Fuggles	35g (1¼oz)	90 minutes
UK Goldings	20g (¾oz)	15 minutes from end
Protofloc	1 teaspoon	15 minutes from end
Boil duration	1½ hours	
Yeast	West Yorkshire Ale—WY-1469	
Target FG	1014	
Target ABV	5.6%	

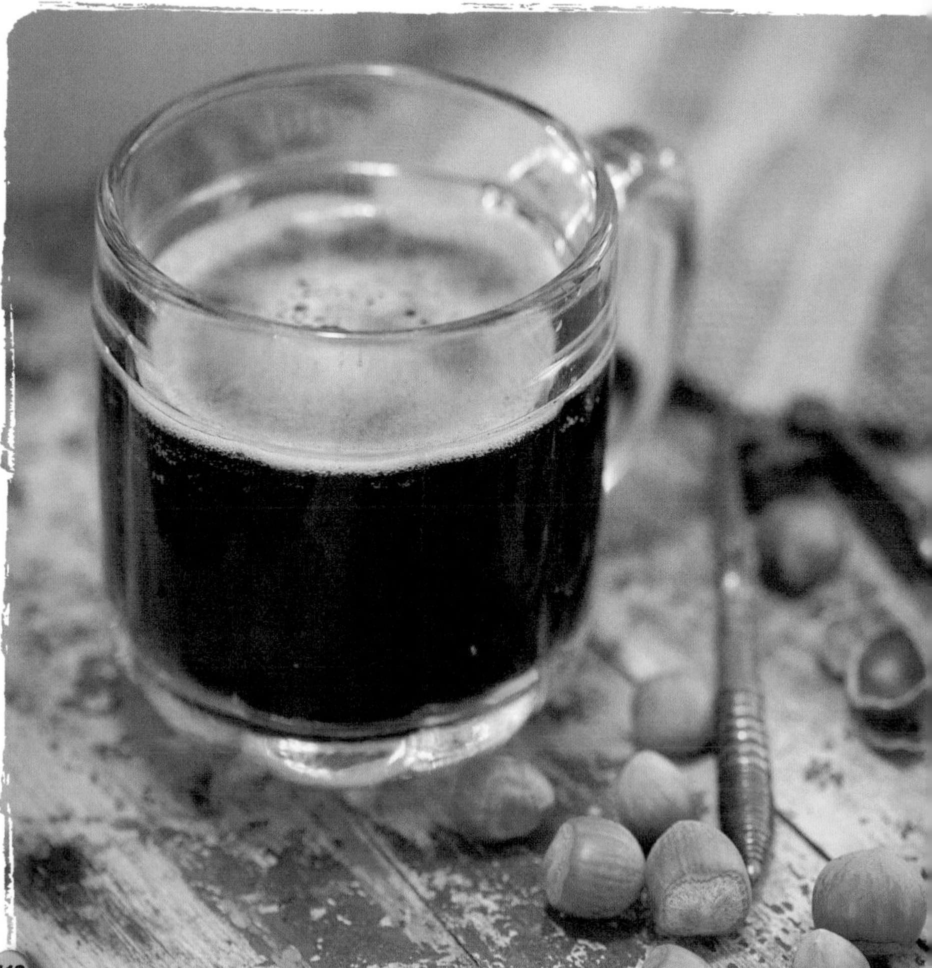

PORTER

First popular in the 1800s, porter (which isn't as rich as stout) is the result of using pale malts and black malt.

Original gravity	1049	
Water	23 litres/5 gallons/6 US gallons	
Mash Roll	**Weight**	
Pale ale malt	4.30g (9½lb)	
Medium crystal malt	425g (15oz)	
Torrified wheat	380g (13½oz)	
Roasted barley	240g (8½oz)	
Mash Schedule	1 hour	
In the Boil	**Weight**	**Time**
Williamette	21g (¾oz)	90 minutes
UK Progress	8g (¼oz)	45 minutes from end
UK Fuggles	15g (½oz)	10 minutes from end
Protofloc	1 teaspoon	15 minutes from end
Boil duration	1½ hours	
Yeast	Irish ale—WY-1084	
Target FG	1013	
Target ABV	4.8%	

A WORD TO THE WISE

Porters make a great base for a variety of further flavors to be introduced. You could try coffee, chocolate, fruit, and spices. A real treat for the brewing brave!

STOUT

The development of stouts and porters is closely linked. Their huge popularity meant that a wide variety of strengths became available. Breweries would often advertise these differing strengths with words like "extra" and "double." Although not universal, these words are the ones that are most commonly used when describing dark beers. Stout porters are those beers with a high gravity, usually 7–8% ABV. Irish stouts, such as Guinness, are best described as dry stouts.

Original gravity	1045	
Water	23 litres/5 gallons/6 US gallons	
Mash Roll	Weight	
Pale ale malt	4.45kg (9¾lb)	
Roasted barley	465g (16½oz)	
Mash Schedule	1 hour	
In the Boil	Weight	Time
UK Target	25g (¾oz)	90 minutes
UK Goldings	12g (½oz)	10 minutes from end
Protofloc	1 teaspoon	15 minutes from end
Boil duration	1½ hours	
Yeast	London ale—WY-1026	
Target FG	1011	
Target ABV	4.6%	

A WORD TO THE WISE

Try adding 70g (2½oz) of cocoa powder and 30g (1oz) of dried chili flakes at the end of the boil. If you fancy giving this a try, also add 5g (⅛oz) of Fuggles hops to even things out.

"When I read about the evils of drinking, I gave up reading."

HENRY YOUNGMAN (1906-1998)

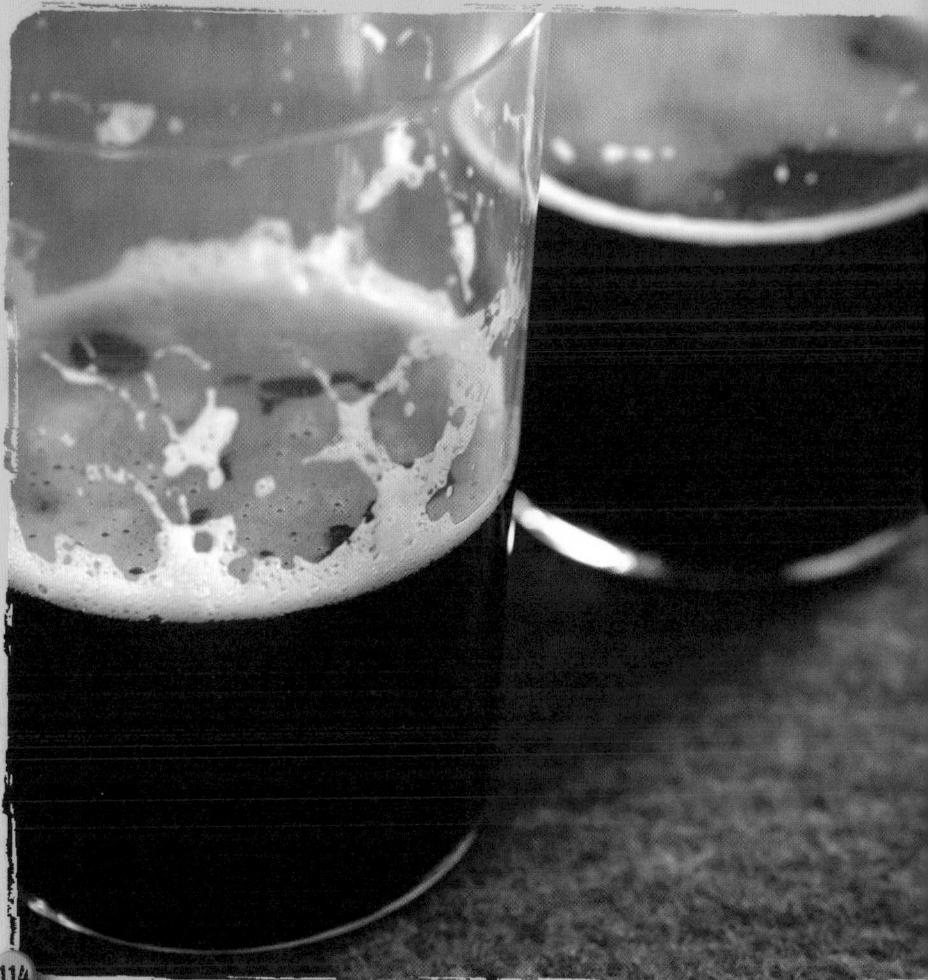

CHOCOLATE STOUT

Malt that is kilned until it has developed a chocolate flavor is used in this brew along with cocoa powder. Some brewers will use adjuncts, such as chocolate nibs, as well as flavorings, such as cranberry, blackberry, and instant coffee, or even make the beer into a double chocolate stout. However, chocolate stout can only be classified as such if chocolate has been added to the brew (and not if the chocolate flavor comes from the malt).

Original gravity	1043	
Water	23 litres/5 gallons/6 US gallons	
Mash Roll	Weight	
Maris otter	3.6kg (8lb)	
Chocolate malt	420g (14¾oz)	
Torrified wheat	260g (9oz)	
Roasted barley	195g (6¾oz)	
Caramunich III	200g (7oz)	
Mash Schedule	1 hour	
In the Boil	Weight	Time
Northern Brewer	38g (1⅛oz)	90 minutes
Cocoa powder	50g (1¾oz)	15 minutes from end
Protofloc	1 teaspoon	15 minutes from end
Boil duration	1½ hours	
Yeast	American ale—WY-1056	
Target FG	1011	
Target ABV	4%	

OATMEAL STOUT

Oatmeal Stout was once considered restorative and nourishing because of the oatmeal used in the mash.

Original gravity	1062
Water	23 litres/5 gallons/6 US gallons

Mash Roll	Weight
2-row malt	3.8kg (8¼lb)
Special B	340g (12oz)
Chocolate malt	226g (8oz)
Carafa II	340g (12oz)
Roasted barley	226g (8oz)
Pale wheat malt	226g (8oz)
Oat flakes	453g (1lb)

Mash Schedule	1½ hours

in the boil	Weight	time
Pacific Gem	14g (½oz)	60 minutes
Hallertauer	28g (1oz)	15 minutes from end
Hallertauer	14g (½oz)	5 minutes from end
Protofloc	1 teaspoon	15 minutes from end

Boil duration	1 hour
Yeast	Irish ale—WY-1084
Target FG	1012
Target ABV	6.5%

COFFEE STOUT

<mark>Dark roasted malts are used in this stout to lend a bitter, coffee flavor alongside ground or instant coffee.</mark>

Original gravity	1086
Water	23 litres/5 gallons/6 US gallons

mash roll	Weight
Maris otter	5.4kg (12lb)
Torrified wheat	453g (1lb)
Chocolate malt	226g (8oz)
Roasted barley	226g (8oz)
Dark crystal malt	453g (1lb)
Coarsely ground coffee beans	226g (8oz)

Mash Schedule	1½ hours

In the Boil	weight	time
Northern Brewer	56g (2oz)	60 minutes
Galena	28g (1oz)	30 minutes from end
Spalt	28g (1oz)	5 minutes from end

Boil duration	1 hour
Yeast	Belgian ale—WY-1388
Target FG	1018
Target ABV	8.5%

A WORD TO THE WISE

For Coffee Stout, you will need two-thirds of a cup of dry malt extract and 3 tablespoons of dark roasted instant coffee. Bottle-condition for at least a month.

SMOKED PORTER

A roasted bitterness is the goal here with a smoky nose: dried fruit, coffee, and chocolate all in one.

Original gravity	1056
Water	23 litres/5 gallons/6 US gallons

Mash Roll	Weight
2-row pale malt	3.1kg (6¾lb)
Caramalt	453g (1lb)
Smoked malt	453g (1lb)
Carapils	340g (12oz)
Wheat malt	226g (8oz)
Chocolate malt	226g (8oz)
Black malt	58g (2oz)

Mash Schedule	1 hour

In the Boil	Weight	Time
Northern Brewer	21g (¾oz)	60 minutes
Williamette	14g (½oz)	15 minutes from end
Williamette	14g (½oz)	at flame-out
Protofloc	1 teaspoon	15 minutes from end

Boil duration	1 hour
Yeast	American ale—WY-1056
Target FG	1014
Target ABV	5.4%

"The problem with the world is that everyone is a few drinks behind."
HUMPHREY BOGART (1899–1957)

BARLEY WINE

Barley Wine was a seasonal beer, historically brewed at harvest time using only the freshest malts and copious amounts of Kent Goldings hops. Barley Wine made from grain rather than fruit is actually a beer!

Original gravity	1098	
Water	23 litres/5 gallons/6 US gallons	
Mash Roll	Weight	
Maris otter malt	4.26kg (9¼lb)	
Medium crystal malt	820g (1¾lb)	
Mash Schedule	1 hour	
In the Boil	Weight	Time
Light liquid malt extract	3kg (6½lb)	90 minutes
Light brown sugar	580g (1¼lb)	90 minutes
Dark brown sugar	350g (12¼oz)	90 minutes
Northdown	46g (1½oz)	90 minutes
UK Goldings	15g (½oz)	10 minutes from end
Protofloc	1 teaspoon	15 minutes from end
Boil duration	1½ hours	
Yeast	British ale—WY-1098	
Target FG	1015	
Target ABV	11.2%	

A WORD TO THE WISE

If we were to use a full-grain recipe for this Barley Wine, the total grain weight would be 8.19kg (18lb)!

WEISSBIER

This beer is also sometimes known as Weizenbier. Weissbier is a Bavarian specialty beer and, according to German law, any weissbiers that are brewed in Germany must be top-fermented. This German beer is highly distinctive in that it has exotic banana and clove notes. These flavors are achieved in the beer as a by-product of fermentation and are what you are aiming for when brewing the beer. You will also be looking out for a generous head of foam.

Original gravity	1056	
Water	23 litres/5 gallons/6 US gallons	
Mash Roll	Weight	
Pale wheat malt	2.4kg (5¼lb)	
Pilsner malt	2kg (4½lb)	
Carapils	226g (8oz)	
Rice hulls	226g (8oz)	
Mash Schedule	1 hour	
In the Boil	Weight	Time
Hallertauer Hersbrucker	23g (¾oz)	60 minutes
Tettnanger	14g (½oz)	15 minutes from end
Protofloc	1 teaspoon	15 minutes from end
Boil duration	1 hour	
Yeast	Weihenstephan Weizen—WY-3068	
Target FG	1014	
Target ABV	5.5%	

RAUCHBIER

Meaning simply "smoked beer," this is an unusual beer style. Rauchbiers are incredibly hard to come by today.

Original gravity	1050
Water	23 litres/5 gallons/6 US gallons

Mash Roll	Weight
Rauch malt	3.24kg (7lb)
Vienna malt	1.16kg (2½lb)
Munich malt	1.16kg (2½lb)
Chocolate malt	230g (8oz)

Mash Schedule	1 hour

In the Boil	Weight	Time
Sterling	16g (½oz)	60 minutes
Czech Saaz	28g (1oz)	15 minutes from end
Crystal	28g (1oz)	10 minutes from end
Protofloc	1 teaspoon	15 minutes from end

Boil duration	1 hour
Yeast	Bavarian lager—WY-2206
Target FG	1013
Target ABV	4.9%

"Not all chemicals are bad. Without chemicals such as hydrogen and oxygen, for example, there would be no way to make water, a vital ingredient in beer."

DAVE BARRY (B.1947)

A WORD TO THE WISE

Before the advent of modern technology, green malt for brewing was dried over an open fire, giving the malt a smoky aroma. So, use Rauch hops to give beer a traditional, smoky flavor.

A WORD TO THE WISE

If you have a sweet palate, opt for a Helles Beer because it is less bitter than a Pilsner.

HELLES BEER

"Helles" means "light one" in German and this brew is indeed a light, straw-colored blonde beer. It is both sparkling and light, but do not be fooled because this really is a full-bodied brew. Light refers only to the subtle coloring and not to the alcoholic strength, which packs quite a punch. A Helles Beer should have a mild, malty flavor in the finish and should also be dry with a dilatory note of hops.

Original gravity	1048	
Water	23 litres/5 gallons/6 US gallons	
Mash Roll	**Weight**	
German 2-row Pilsner malt	3.6kg (8lb)	
Munich malt	113g (4oz)	
Carafoam	340g (12oz)	
German Vienna malt	340g (12oz)	
Mash Schedule	1 hour	
In the Boil	**Weight**	**Time**
Hallertauer Mittelfrueh	31g (1oz)	60 minutes
Hallertauer Mittelfrueh	15g (½oz)	15 minutes from end
Czech Saaz	15g (½oz)	1 minute from end
Protofloc	1 teaspoon	15 minutes from end
Boil duration	1 hour	
Yeast	Bohemian lager—WY-2124	
Target FG	1010	
Target ABV	5%	

ROGGENBIER
A specialty beer originating from Bavaria, with dominant grain flavors and a rich, creamy white head.

Original gravity	1034
Water	23 litres/5 gallons/6 US gallons

Mash Roll	Weight
2-row pale malt	3.9kg (8½lb)
Cararye	1kg (2¼lb)
Light crystal malt	481g (17oz)

Mash Schedule	1 hour

In the Boil	Weight	Time
Tettnanger	21g (¾oz)	60 minutes
Hallertauer Mittlefreuh	14g (½oz)	30 minutes from end
Saaz	12g (½oz)	30 minutes from end
Hallertauer Mittlefreuh	12g (½oz)	5 minutes from end
Saaz	14g (½oz)	5 minutes from end
Protofloc	1 teaspoon	15 minutes from end

Boil duration	1 hour
Yeast	Bavarian wheat—WY-3638
Target FG	1008
Target ABV	4.5%

BOCK BEER

This is a heavy, malty brew. Incredibly smooth, it is not one to knock back, but to sip, savor, and enjoy.

Original gravity	1067
Water	23 litres/5 gallons/6 US gallons

Mash Roll	Weight
German Pils malt	2.7kg (6lb)
Dark Munich malt	1.3kg (2¾lb)
Light Munich malt	1.3kg (2¾lb)
Caramunich II	340g (12oz)
Belgian special B	113g (4oz)
German carafa special II	56g (2oz)

Mash Schedule	1 hour

In the Boil	Weight	Time
Hallertauer	14g (½oz)	90 minutes
Magnum	7g (¼oz)	60 minutes from end
Hallertauer	21g (¾oz)	60 minutes from end
Hallertauer	14g (½oz)	10 minutes from end
Protofloc	1 teaspoon	15 minutes from end

Boil duration	1½ hours
Yeast	Bohemian lager—WY-2124
Target FG	1015
Target ABV	5.5%

DOPPELBOCK

Released for the first time in 1780, "double bock" is so called because of the large quantity of grain to water.

Original gravity	1072	
Water	23 litres/5 gallons/6 US gallons	
Mash Roll	Weight	
Pilsner malt	4.25kg (9¼lb)	
Munich I	1.1kg (2½lb)	
Lager malt	662g (1½lb)	
Dark crystal malt	449g (1lb)	
Chocolate malt	90g (3oz)	
Mash Schedule	1 hour	
In the Boil	Weight	Time
Crystal	13g (½oz)	60 minutes
Tettnanger	28g (1oz)	60 minutes
Crystal	28g (1oz)	30 minutes from end
Protofloc	1 teaspoon	15 minutes from end
Boil duration	1 hour	
Yeast	Munich lager—WY-2308	
Target FG	1018	
Target ABV	7.2%	

KELLERBIER

This beer is renowned for being served before dinner as an appetite stimulant. It means "cellar beer" and is highly flavored with aromatic hops. Kellerbier has a great amber color because it contains caramalized malt. It would normally be matured unbunged in a wooden barrel, typically with very little effervescence. For this reason, not much in the way of a foamy head is formed when the beer is poured into the glass.

Original gravity	1051	
Water	23 litres/5 gallons/6 US gallons	
Mash Roll	Weight	
German 2-row Pilsner malt	3.6kg (8lb)	
Munich malt	1.8kg (4lb)	
Chocolate malt	113g (4oz)	
Mash Schedule	1 hour	
In the Boil	Weight	Time
Saaz	56g (2oz)	75 minutes
Hallertauer Hersbrucker	28g (4oz)	10 minutes from end
Protofloc	1 teaspoon	15 minutes from end
Boil duration	1¼ hours	
Yeast	German ale—WY-1007	
Target FG	1013	
Target ABV	5.2%	

KÖLLSCH

This is the German version of a British pale ale. Traditionally brewed in Cologne, it is one of the palest German beers and one of only a handful of traditional German ales. Apparently, Kolsch is the only language that you can drink, as the word "kollsch" means "Cologne-ish," the local dialect. It is a subtle and delicate brew, making it a fantastic beer for summer quaffing.

Original gravity	1046	
Water	23 litres/5 gallons/6 US gallons	
Mash Roll	Weight	
German wheat malt	1.1kg (2½lb)	
Munich malt	1.1kg (2½lb)	
German 2-row Pilsner malt	1kg (2¼lb)	
Vienna malt	1kg (2¼lb)	
Carapils	935g (2lb)	
Mash Schedule	1 hour	
In the Boil	Weight	Time
Tettnanger	28g (1oz)	60 minutes
Hallertauer	14g (½oz)	30 minutes from end
Czech Saaz	14g (½oz)	5 minutes from end
Czech Saaz	14g (½oz)	1 minute from end
Hallertauer	14g (½oz)	1 minute from end
Protofloc	1 teaspoon	15 minutes from end
Boil duration	1 hour	
Yeast	Kolsch—WY- 2565	
Target FG	1008	
Target ABV	5.1%	

HEFEWEIZEN

This is a beer style that is usually full-bodied, fruity, and sweet. Hefeweizens are lightly hopped and made with an equal quantity of barley and wheat malts. You may notice a yeast sediment with this beer, so pour your brew with care unless you enjoy the cloudiness created by the yeast. This is a top-fermented and bottle-conditioned beer.

Original gravity	1048	
Water	23 litres/5 gallons/6 US gallons	
Mash Roll	Weight	
German Pilsner malt	2.5kg (5½lb)	
German wheat malt	2.5kg (5½lb)	
Mash Schedule	1 hour	
In the Boil	Weight	Time
Hallertauer Hersbrucker	35g (1¼oz)	60 minutes
Hallertauer Hersbrucker	7g (¼oz)	15 minutes from end
Hallertauer Hersbrucker	14g (½oz)	5 minutes from end
Protofloc	1 teaspoon	15 minutes from end
Boil duration	1 hour	
Yeast	Weihenstephen Weizen—WY-3068	
Target FG	1008	
Target ABV	4.3%	

A WORD TO THE WEIZEN

Wheat beers such as Hefeweizen were orginally banned by the German Purity Laws because they contained ingredients other than malted barley, hops and water.

OKTOBERFEST

Originating in Bavaria, this beer is an adaptation of Viennese lager with a higher alcohol level, producing a noticeable (if low) hop bitterness. Traditionally brewed in March, this beer is matured in cellar caves in readiness for the fall festivities, known as the Oktoberfest, which take place in Munich, Bavaria, in late September. This beer festival has become an important date in the German calendar since the first event was held in 1810.

Original gravity	1062	
Water	23 litres/5 gallons/6 US gallons	
Mash Roll	Weight	
Vienna malt	3.6kg (8lb)	
Munich malt	453g (1lb)	
Caramel malt	226g (8oz)	
Pilsner malt	226g (8oz)	
Mash Schedule	1 hour	
In the Boil	Weight	Time
Tettnanger	28g (1oz)	60 minutes
Saaz	28g (1oz)	30 minutes from end
Protofloc	1 teaspoon	15 minutes from end
Boil duration	1 hour	
Yeast	Octoberfest lager blend—WY-2633	
Target FG	1015	
Target ABV	5.7%	

DUNKLES

Meaning simply "dark" beer, this is a full-bodied beer which has a fantastic, nutty, rounded finish.

Original gravity	1048
Water	23 litres/5 gallons/6 US gallons

Mash Roll	Weight
German wheat malt	1.7kg (3¾lb)
German 2-row Pilsner malt	1.3kg (2¾lb)
Vienna malt	680g (1½lb)
Munich malt	453g (1lb)
Caramunich	285g (10oz)
Chocolate malt	27g (1oz)

Mash Schedule	1 hour

In the Boil	Weight	Time
Tettnanger	40g (1½oz)	60 minutes
Hallertau Hersbrucker	8g (¼oz)	15 minutes from end
Protofloc	1 teaspoon	15 minutes from end

Boil duration	1 hour
Yeast	Bavarian wheat—WY- 3638
Target FG	1010
Target ABV	5.4%

SCHWARZBIER

Meaning "black beer," this brew has a clean lager taste and great tones of chocolate, coffee, and vanilla.

Original gravity	1054
Water	23 litres/5 gallons/6 US gallons

Mash Roll	Weight
Munich malt	2kg (4½lb)
Vienna malt	2kg (4½lb)
Munich dark malt	453g (1lb)
Carafa III	226g (8oz)
Caramunich	226g (8oz)

Mash Schedule	1 hour

In the Boil	Weight	Time
Perle	28g (1oz)	65 minutes
Perle	28g (1oz)	10-day dry hop

Boil duration	1 hour 5 minutes
Yeast	Bavarian lager—WY- 2206
Target FG	1014
Target ABV	4.8%

"Give me a woman who loves beer and I will conquer the world."

KAISER WILHELM II (1859-1941)

PALE ALE

This is one of the world's most popular beer styles, with a high proportion of pale malts giving rise to a lighter color.

Original gravity	1045	
Water	23 litres/5 gallons/6 US gallons	
Mash Roll	**Weight**	
2-row pale malt	3.8kg (8¼lb)	
Carapils	226g (8oz)	
Light crystal malt	226g (8oz)	
Mash Schedule	1 hour	
In the Boil	**Weight**	**Time**
Amarillo	14g (½oz)	60 minutes
Amarillo	14g (½oz)	15 minutes from end
Citra	28g (1oz)	15 minutes from end
Amarillo	28g (1oz)	1 minute from end
Citra	28g (1oz)	1 minute from end
Amarillo	28g (1oz)	14-day dry hop
Protofloc	1 teaspoon	15 minutes from end
Boil duration	1 hour	
Yeast	American ale—WY-1056	
Target FG	1010	
Target ABV	4.5%	

STEAM BEER

The name for "steam beer" is perplexing since there is no definite source for it. Some say the name arose because it was made with lager yeasts at high temperatures, which made it so effervescent that it needed to let off steam! Other sources suggest it was a German variety of beer called "Dampfbier," perhaps used by American brewers of German descent. Once known for being inexpensive and of low-quality, it has now been reinvented as a craft beer.

Original gravity	1049	
Water	23 litres/5 gallons/6 US gallons	
Mash Roll	Weight	
Pale ale malt	4.5kg (9¾lb)	
Caramel malt	136g (4¾oz)	
Carapils	123g (4¼oz)	
Mash Schedule	1 hour	
In the Boil	Weight	Time
Northern Brewer	38g (1¼oz)	60 minutes
Northern Brewer	13g (½oz)	15 minutes from end
Northern Brewer	17g (½oz)	5 minutes from end
Protofloc	1 teaspoon	15 minutes from end
Boil duration	1 hour	
Yeast	California lager—WY-2112	
Target FG	1015	
Target ABV	4.5%	

A WORD TO THE WISE

Steam Beer has strong associations with California and sometimes goes by the name of California Common Beer.

A WORD TO THE WISE

In Cream Ale, honey can be used instead of sugar but it needs to be put in at flame-out in the boil stage.

CREAM ALE

This is a light, crisp ale that is perfect for drinking in the summer. Some cream ales have plentiful hop characters. Interestingly, cream ale was once a pre-prohibition ale in the United States, and came in two distinguishable varieties. These were Dark Common Beer and Regular Cream Common Beer. Now the ale is cold-conditioned to give its nice clean finish.

Original gravity	1057	
Water	23 litres/5 gallons/6 US gallons	
Mash Roll	Weight	
Pilsner malt	1.5kg (3¼lb)	
2-row pale malt	1.5kg (3¼lb)	
Flaked corn	227g (8oz)	
Sugar	227g (8oz)	
Mash Schedule	1¼ hours	
In the Boil	Weight	Time
Liberty	23g (¾oz)	60 minutes
Liberty	8g (¼oz)	1 minute from end
Protofloc	1 teaspoon	15 minutes from end
Boil duration	1 hour	
Yeast	American ale—WY-1056	
Target FG	1010	
Target ABV	5.4%	

MILK STOUT

Sweet and smooth, this brew is a great introduction to the world of heavier beers, such as traditional stouts and porters. Do not be misled by the name, however. This beer does not contain any milk. Instead, lactose (the sugar that is found in milk) is added at the end of the boiling stage. You should find that the lactose will take the edge off the bitterness that is typical of many stouts and porters, leaving you with a deliciously smooth beer.

Original gravity	1062	
Water	23 litres/5 gallons/6 US gallons	

Mash Roll	Weight	
2-row pale malt	3kg (6½lb)	
Roasted barley	460g (1lb)	
Medium crystal malt	340g (12oz)	
Chocolate malt	340g (12oz)	
Munich malt	340g (12oz)	
Flaked barley	283g (10oz)	
Flaked oats	226g (8oz)	

Mash Schedule	1½ hours	

In the Boil	Weight	Time
Magnum	10g (¼oz)	60 minutes
Goldings	28g (1oz)	10 minutes from end
Protofloc	1 teaspoon	15 minutes from end
Lactose	460g (1lb)	10 minutes from end

Boil duration	1 hour	
Yeast	Irish ale—WY-1084	
Target FG	1022	
Target ABV	5%	

"I am a firm
believer in
the people.
If given
the truth,
they can be
depended upon
to meet any
national crisis.
The great point
is to bring them
the real facts,
and beer."

ABRAHAM LINCOLN
(1809-1865)

149

"Beer is proof that God loves us and wants us to be happy."

BENJAMIN FRANKLIN
(1706-1790)

DOUBLE STOUT
Full-bodied and packed with rich flavors, American Double Stouts are strong on both alcohol and taste.

Original gravity	1123
Water	23 litres/5 gallons/6 US gallons

Mash Roll	Weight
Pale malt	11.5kg (25¼ lb)
Crystal malt (dark)	1.8kg (4lb)
Chocolate malt	910g (2lb)
Roasted wheat	453g (1lb)
Crystal malt (dark)	453g (1lb)
Black patent malt	226g (8oz)
Pale chocolate malt	226g (8oz)
Belgian kiln coffee malt	226g (8oz)

Mash Schedule	1½ hours

In the Boil	Weight	Time
Northern Brewer	28g (1oz)	60 minutes
Williamette	28g (1oz)	60 minutes
Magnum	28g (1oz)	60 minutes
Williamette	28g (1oz)	15 minutes from end
Protofloc	1 teaspoon	15 minutes from end

Boil duration	1 hour
Yeast	American ale—WY-1056
Target FG	1032
Target ABV	12%

PALE LAGER

American pale lagers are made from an all-malt mash, so have a stronger malt flavor than those made with rice or corn.

Original gravity	1050	
Water	23 litres/5 gallons/6 US gallons	
Mash Roll	Weight	
2-row pale malt	4kg (8¾lb)	
Dark crystal malt	311g (11oz)	
Carapils	57g (2oz)	
Mash Schedule	1 hour	
In the Boil	Weight	Time
Columbus	24g (¾oz)	85 minutes
Cascade	21g (¾oz)	30 minutes from end
Cascade	23g (¾oz)	5 minutes from end
Cascade	23g (¾oz)	at flame-out
Protofloc	1 teaspoon	15 minutes from end
Cascade	14g (½oz)	dry-hop after 5 days
Boil duration	1 hour 25 minutes	
Yeast	American lager—WY-2035	
Target FG	1010	
Target ABV	5.5%	

A WORD TO THE WISE

You can keep down the cost of brewing a pale lager by using adjuncts such as corn and rice, although some pale lagers are adjunct-free and will have a more robust level of malt and hops.

AMBER ALE

American amber ales have a stronger caramel flavor and are darker in color than pale ales.

Original gravity	1046
Water	23 litres/5 gallons/6 US gallons

Mash Roll	Weight
2-row pale malt	2.4kg (5¼lb)
Caramel malt	1kg (2¼lb)
Munich malt	910g (2lb)
Biscuit malt	226g (8oz)
Wheat malt	113g (4oz)

Mash Schedule	1 hour	

In the Boil	Weight	Time
Amarillo	28g (1oz)	60 minutes
Centennial	14g (½oz)	15 minutes from end

Boil duration	1 hour
Yeast	American ale—WY-1056
Target FG	1012
Target ABV	4.8%

GOLDEN ALE As the name suggests, an American golden ale will be copper in color. It is lighter in body than typical pale ales.

Original gravity	1059	
Water	23 litres/5 gallons/6 US gallons	
Mash Roll 2-row malt Pilsen malt Munich malt	Weight 2.3kg (5lb) 1.8kg (4lb) 907g (2lb)	
Mash Schedule	1 hour	
In the Boil Cascade Cascade Williamette Amarillo Williamette Protofloc	Weight 14g (½oz) 35g (1¼oz) 28g (1oz) 28g (1oz) 7g (¼oz) 1 teaspoon	Time 60 minutes 30 minutes from end 20 minutes from end 10 minutes from end 10 minutes from end 15 minutes from end
Boil duration	1 hour	
Yeast	American ale II—WY-1272	
Target FG	1015	
Target ABV	5.9%	

A WORD TO THE WISE

The Cascade hops in Summer IPA help to give this brew a fresh citrus flavor that is reminiscent of grapefruit. It's perfect for relaxed summer drinking.

SUMMER IPA
A rich copper in color and bursting with citrusy aromas and tastes, this is a thirst-quenching summer brew.

Original gravity	1066	
Water	23 litres/5 gallons/6 US gallons	

Mash Roll	Weight	
2-row pale malt	6kg (13¼lb)	
Medium crystal malt	226g (8oz)	
Carapils	226g (8oz)	

Mash Schedule	1 hour	

In the Boil	Weight	Time
Magnum	14g (½oz)	60 minutes
Williamette	14g (½oz)	45 minutes from end
Cascade	28g (1oz)	20 minutes from end
Amarillo	28g (1oz)	10 minutes from end
Amarillo	28g (1oz)	5 minutes from end
Cascade	28g (1oz)	5 minutes from end
Amarillo	28g (1oz)	at flame-out
Protofloc	1 teaspoon	15 minutes from end

Boil duration	1 hour	
Yeast	American ale—WY-1056	
Target FG	1012	
Target ABV	5%	

STRONG ALE
A potent alcohol content is one of the distinguishing characteristics of the American stong-ale style.

Original gravity	1103	
Water	23 litres/5 gallons/6 US gallons	
Mash Roll	**Weight**	
2-row pale malt	8.2kg (18lb)	
Special B	566g (1¼lb)	
Honey malt	340g (12oz)	
Wheat malt	340g (12oz)	
2-row black malt	340g (12oz)	
Mash Schedule	1½ hours	
In the Boil	**Weight**	**Time**
Chinook	28g (1oz)	60 minutes
Perle	28g (1oz)	30 minutes from end
Williamette	56g (2oz)	1 minute from end
Protofloc	1 teaspoon	15 minutes from end
Boil duration	1 hour	
Yeast	American ale—WY-1056	
Target FG	1020	
Target ABV	11%	

CASCADE ALE
The name of this ale comes from Cascade, a type of hops, which provides the citrus and grapefruit flavors.

Original gravity	1045	
Water	23 litres/5 gallons/6 US gallons	
Mash Roll	Weight	
Pilsner malt	5kg (11lb)	
Torrified wheat	226g (8oz)	
Mash Schedule	1 hour	
In the Boil	Weight	Time
Cascade	15g (½oz)	60 minutes
Saaz	15g (½oz)	30 minutes from end
Cascade	31g (1oz)	30 minutes from end
Saaz	15g (½oz)	1 minute from end
Protofloc	1 teaspoon	15 minutes from end
Boil duration	1 hour	
Yeast	Belgian Ardennes—WY-3522	
Target FG	1010	
Target ABV	4%	

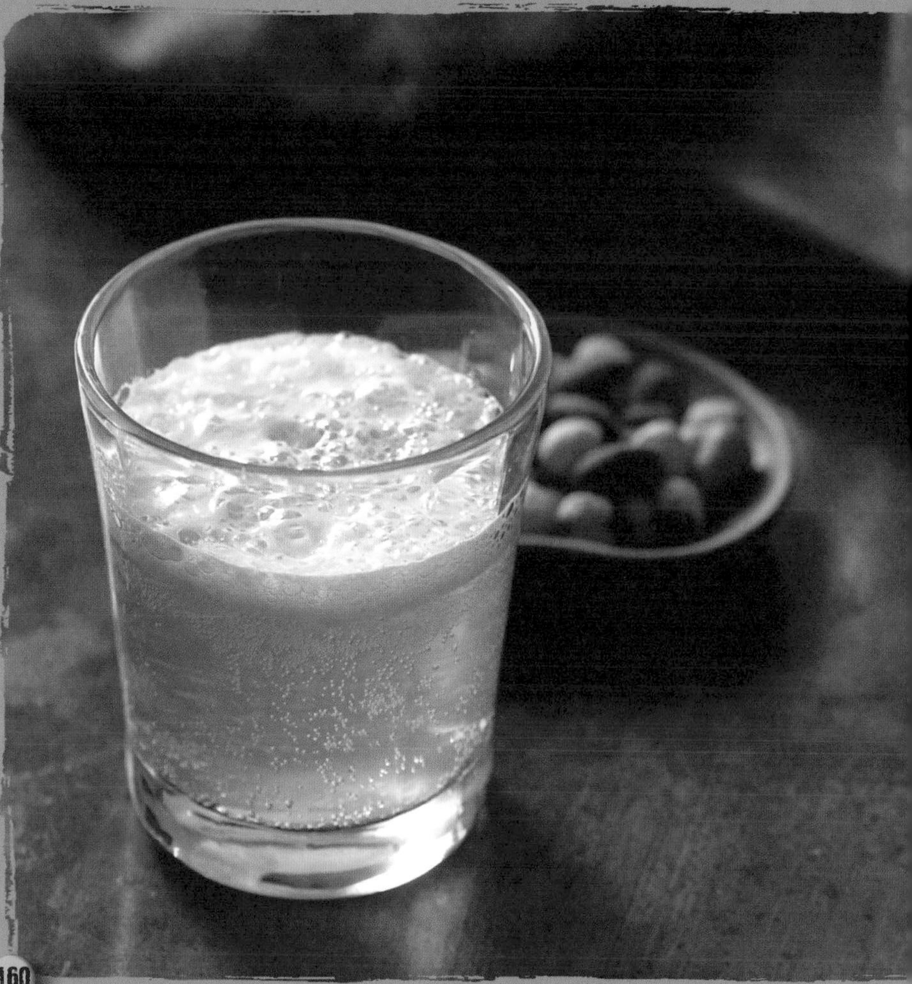

CITRA SPECIAL
Indulge in the exotic-fruit aromas and flavors imparted by the Citra hops to this rather special beer.

Original gravity	1045	
Water	23 litres/5 gallons/6 US gallons	

Mash Roll	Weight	
2-row pale malt	3.8kg (8¼lb)	
Carapils	226g (8oz)	
Light crystal malt	226g (8oz)	

Mash Schedule	1 hour	

In the Boil	Weight	Time
Citra	14g (½oz)	60 minutes
Amarillo	14g (½oz)	15 minutes from end
Citra	28g (1oz)	15 minutes from end
Amarillo	28g (1oz)	1 minute from end
Citra	28g (1oz)	1 minute from end
Protofloc	1 teaspoon	15 minutes from end
Citra	28g (1oz)	14-day dry hop

Boil duration	1 hour	
Yeast	American ale—WY-1056	
Target FG	1010	
Target ABV	4.5%	

BOURBON BEER

Brewery version of this beer use whiskey barrels to impart the flavor of the bourbon—not a piece of kit that many homebrewers own. Luckily, French oak beans soaked in bourbon will give the brew that familiar woody flavor.

Original gravity	1071	
Water	23 litres/5 gallons/6 US gallons	
Mash Roll	**Weight**	
2-row malt	2.7kg (6lb)	
Pilsen malt	2.7kg (6lb)	
Biscuit malt	226g (8oz)	
Crystal malt medium	453g (1lb)	
Honey malt	226g (8oz)	
Brown sugar	453g (1lb)	
Mash Schedule	1 hour	
In the Boil	**Weight**	**Time**
Centennial	9g (¼oz)	60 minutes
Chinook	7g (¼oz)	45 minutes from end
Amarillo	14g (½oz)	30 minutes from end
Liberty	28g (1oz)	15 minutes from end
Nugget	14g (½oz)	15 minutes from end
Cascade	14g (½oz)	2 minutes from end
Protofloc	1 teaspoon	15 minutes from end
Cascade	28g (1oz)	dry hop
French oak beans	56g (2oz)	14-day secondary fermenter
Boil duration	1 hour	
Yeast	California lager—WY-2112	
Target FG	1020	
Target ABV	6%	

A WORD TO THE WISE

You'll need to soak the French oak beans in bourbon for 2 months before starting the recipe, adding 28g (1oz) of Colombus hops 3 weeks from the end of the soaking time.

Chapter 5

FRUIT BEERS

STRAWBERRY BEER

There has been an explosion of interest in fruit-flavored beers in recent years. One of the most popular of these is Strawberry Beer. You will need to add quite a few pounds of strawberries to this fruit-driven Belgian beer, but this takes place at secondary fermentation stage. It is surprisingly light given its strength. Your beer should have a distinctive strawberry aroma, a rose-pink hue, and a head that disappears when poured.

Original gravity	1048	
Water	23 litres/5 gallons/6 US gallons	
Mash Roll	Weight	
Torrified wheat	2.48kg (5½lb)	
Pilsner malt	2.48kg (5½lb)	
Mash Schedule	1 hour	
In the Boil	Weight	Time
Fuggles	31g (1oz)	90 minutes
Protofloc	1 teaspoon	15 minutes from end
Frozen strawberries (thawed)	4.53kg (10lb)	in the secondary fermentation
Boil duration	1½ hours	
Yeast	Belgian wheat—WY-3942	
Expected FG	1013	
Expected ABV	4.8%	

CHERRY BEER

Use normal morello cherries as the traditional Belgian cherry called the "krieken" is difficult to find.

Original gravity	1062	
Water	23 litres/5 gallons/6 US gallons	
Mash Roll	Weight	
Lager malt	2.3kg (5lb)	
Wheat malt	2.2kg (4¾lb)	
Mash Schedule	1 hour	
In the Boil	Weight	Time
Northern Brewer	22g (¾oz)	90 minutes
Morello cherries	4kg (8¾lb)	at the end
Protofloc	1 teaspoon	15 minutes from end
Pectolase	20g (¾oz)	in the fermenter
Boil duration	1½ hours	
Yeast	Belgian strong ale—WY-1388	
Target FG	1015	
Target ABV	6.3%	

A WORD TO THE WISE

In Cherry Beer, pectolase is needed to stop the brew from setting like jelly and also to clear the end product.

RASPBERRY BEER

You're looking for a fruity aroma without disturbing the beer balance in taste and a ruby-red hue.

Original gravity	1055	
Water	23 litres/5 gallons/6 US gallons	
Mash Roll	**Weight**	
Pilsner malt	2.49kg (5½lb)	
Wheat malt	2.49kg (5½lb)	
Flaked oats	226g (8oz)	
Mash Schedule	1 hour	
In the Boil	**Weight**	**Time**
Hallertau	28g (1oz)	60 minutes
Protofloc	1 teaspoon	15 minutes from end
Frozen raspberries (thawed)	1.13kg (2½lb)	in the secondary fermentation
Boil duration	1 hour	
Yeast	American ale—WY-1056	
Target FG	1005	
Target ABV	4%	

A WORD TO THE WISE

For Raspberry Beer, rack on to the raspberries in the secondary fermentation and make sure they are frozen because you don't want to be dealing with funky wild yeasts.

PASSION FRUIT BEER

This is fruity and tropical in aroma and dangerously drinkable, with a smooth mouth-feel.

Original gravity	1048	
Water	23 litres/5 Gallons/6 US Gallons	
Mash Roll	Weight	
Wheat malt	2kg (4½lb)	
2-row malt	1.6kg (3½lb)	
Unmalted wheat	450g (1lb)	
Munich malt	225g (8oz)	
Rice hulls	225g (8oz)	
Mash Schedule	1 hour	
In the Boil	Weight	Time
Hallertauer	14g (½oz)	60 minutes
Mt. Hood	14g (½oz)	40 minutes from end
Amarillo	14g (½oz)	5 minutes from end
Passion fruit purée	475ml (16½fl.oz)	5 minutes from end
Mango purée	950ml (33½fl.oz)	5 minutes from end
Protofloc	1 teaspoon	15 minutes from end
Boil duration	1 hour	
Yeast	American ale—WY-1056	
Target FG	1008	
Target ABV	3.6%	

FIG BEER

Rich and complex in flavor, figs are less tart than berries. Vary the brew with dates, raisins, and a little vanilla.

Original gravity	1062	
Water	23 litres/5 gallons/6 US gallons	
Mash Roll	Weight	
Pale malt	4.5kg (9¾lb)	
Carapils	113g (4oz)	
Mash Schedule	1½ hours	
In the Boil	Weight	Time
Amarillo	15g (½oz)	60 minutes
Protofloc	1 teaspoon	15 minutes from end
Fig purée	3.15kg (6¾lb)	in the secondary fermentor for 7 days
Boil duration	1 hour	
Yeast	Irish ale—WY-1084	
Target FG	1010	
TARGET ABV	5.5%	

PEACH BEER

Using real fruit rather than fruit syrup is a taste revelation. Try adding grated ginger to the secondary fermenter.

Original gravity	1065	
Water	23 litres/5 gallons/6 US gallons	
Mash Roll	Weight	
Pale ale malt	2.72kg (6lb)	
Wheat malt	2.72kg (6lb)	
Cara amber	453g (1lb)	
Chocolate malt	113g (4oz)	
Mash Schedule	1 hour	
In the Boil	Weight	Time
Chinook	14g (½oz)	60 minutes
Chinook	14g (½oz)	45 minutes from end
Amarillo	14g (½oz)	30 minutes from end
Cascade	14g (½oz)	15 minutes from end
Mt.Hood	14g (½oz)	at the end
Frozen peaches (thawed)	1.8kg (4lb)	add to secondary fermentation
Protofloc	1 teaspoon	15 minutes from end
Amarillo	28g (1oz)	dry hop for 7 days
Boil duration	1 hour	
Yeast	American ale—WY-1056	
Target FG	1011	
Target ABV	7.5%	

BLACKBERRY STOUT A rich stout, slightly

nutty, with blackberry and coffee aromas. Reaches its prime within 4-6 weeks.

Original gravity	1045	
Water	23 litres/5 gallons/6 US gallons	
Mash Roll	Weight	
Pale ale malt	4.45kg (9¾lb)	
Roasted barley	465g (16½oz)	
Mash Schedule	1 hour	
In the Boil	Weight	Time
UK Target	25g (¾oz)	90 minutes
UK Goldings	12g (½oz)	10 minutes from end
Protofloc	1 teaspoon	15 minutes from end
Frozen blackberries (thawed)	1.18kg (2½lb)	add to secondary fermentation
Boil duration	1½ hours	
Yeast	London ale—WY-1026	
Target FG	1011	
Target ABV	5.3%	

Chapter 6

REST OF THE WORLD BEERS

PILSNER

The Bohemian Pilsner originates from the Czech Republic. First brewed in 1842 in the city of Pilsen, from where it takes its name, Pilsner was then swiftly adapted by German brewers in order to create their own style of beer. This particular Pilsner should be pale gold in color. It should have a strong bitterness on drinking, as well as a clearly noticeable hop presence. As you drink, savor the dryness of the finish.

Original gravity	1045	
Water	23 litres/5 gallons/6 US gallons	
Mash Roll Pilsner malt	Weight 4.75kg (10½lb)	
Mash Schedule	1½hours	
In the Boil Hallertauer Tettnanger Protofloc	Weight 23g (¾oz) 20g (¾oz) 1 teaspoon	Time 90 minutes 10 minutes from end 15 minutes from end
Boil duration	1½ hours	
Yeast	Czech Pilsner—WY-2278	
Expected FG	1011	
Expected ABV	4.5%	

VIENNESE LAGER

Originally developed in Vienna in 1841, this lager should be amber to copper in color and have a lightly bittered hop balance. The presence of Vienna and Munich malts make this lager darker than other lager styles. You may find this lager sold under a different name, Amber Lager, which is just the global interpretation of the Viennese Lager and allows for variation to the malt and hopping ratios.

Original gravity	1049	
Water	23 litres/5 gallons/6 US gallons	
Mash Roll	**Weight**	
Vienna malt	4.7kg (10½lb)	
Munich malt	580g (1¼lb)	
Black malt	50g (1¾oz)	
Mash Schedule	1½ hours	
In the Boil	**Weight**	**Time**
Tettnanger	40g (1½oz)	90 minutes
Saaz	10g (¼oz)	30 minutes from end
Protofloc	1 teaspoon	15 minutes from end
Boil duration	1½ hours	
Yeast	Munich Lager—WY-2308	
Target FG	1012	
Target ABV	5%	

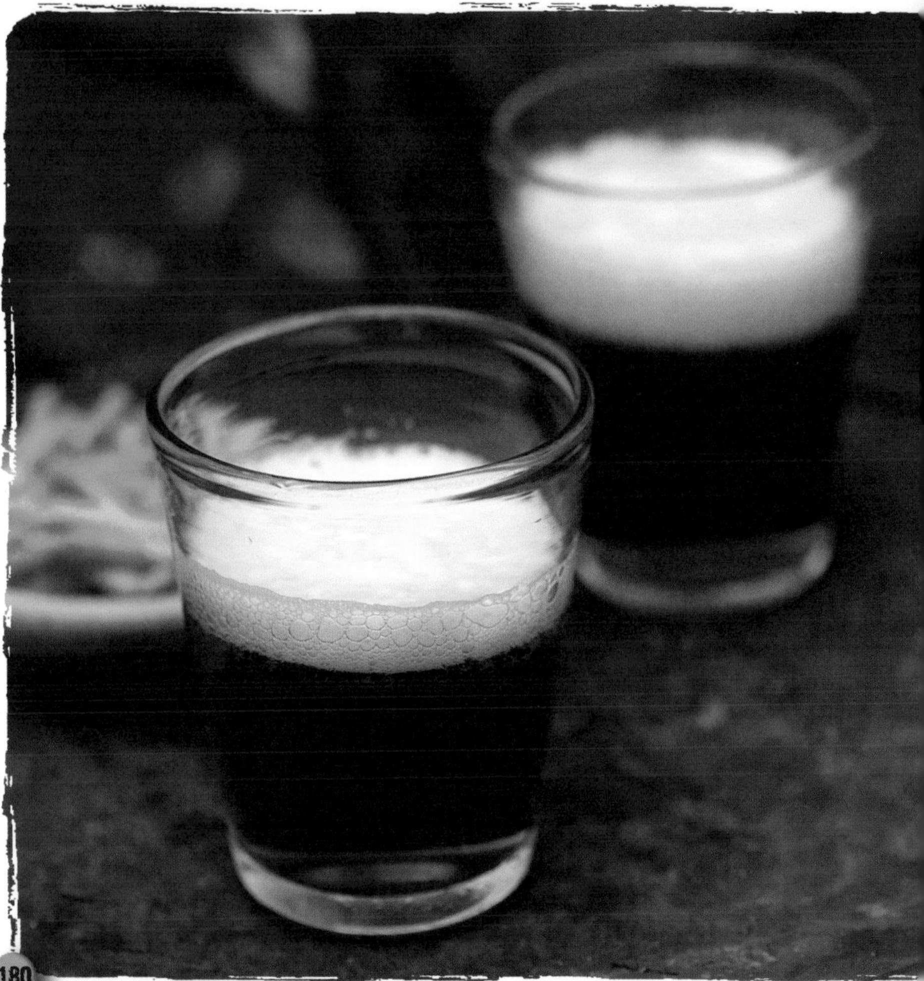

NEW ZEALAND JADE ALE

This is a rich and medium-bodied ale. You should find that the color will be red to brown in varying degrees. The recipe is fairly heavy on the hops like the Imperial Red Ale. This brew should develop a great malty backbone with an equally good hop aroma. If you find that it is just not hoppy enough for your taste, then try adding another 14g (half an ounce) of Pacific Jade hops 5 minutes from the end.

Original gravity	1050	
Water	23 litres/5 gallons/6 US gallons	
Mash Roll	Weight	
Pale malt	2.5kg (5½lb)	
Munich malt	900g (2lb)	
Biscuit malt	226g (8oz)	
Wheat malt	113g (4oz)	
Mash Schedule	1½ hours	
In the Boil	Weight	Time
Pacific Jade	28g (1oz)	60 minutes
Pacific Jade	14g (½oz)	15 minutes from end
Protofloc	1 teaspoon	15 minutes from end
Boil duration	1 hour	
Yeast	American ale—WY-1056	
Target FG	1012	
Target ABV	5%	

BOKKØL

This strong lager is dark in color and also blessed with a powerful caramel characteristic on tasting. This makes it an excellent choice for serving with sweet dishes or desserts at the end of a meal, perhaps as an alternative to drinking port or madeira. Traditionally, this lager was brewed in the fall and then stored in barrels ready for drinking the following spring. It will have a gentle head when poured. You should find that it's as much of a delight to look at as it's a pleasure to drink.

Original gravity	1062
Water	23 litres/5 gallons/6 US gallons

Mash Roll	Weight	
Pilsen malt	2.7kg (6lb)	
Light Munich malt	1.4kg (3lb)	
Carapils	226g (8oz)	
Light crystal malt	453g (1lb)	

Mash Schedule	1½ hours

In the Boil	Weight	Time
Perle	30g (1oz)	60 minutes
Tettnanger	28g (1oz)	20 minutes from end
Hallertauer	28g (1oz)	15 minutes from end
Caraway seeds (crushed)	1 teaspoon	15 minutes from end
Protofloc	1 teaspoon	15 minutes from end

Boil duration	1 hour
Yeast	Bohemian lager—WY-2124
Target FG	1011
Target ABV	7%

GLOSSARY

Adjunct Any non-enzymatic fermentable. Adjuncts include unmalted cereals, such as flaked barley or corn grits, syrups, and sugars.

Aldehyde A chemical precursor to alcohol. In some cases, alcohol can be oxidized to aldehydes, creating off-flavors.

Ale A beer brewed from a top-fermenting yeast with a relatively short, warm fermentation.

Alpha Acid Units (AAU) A home-brewing measurement of hops that quantifies the amount of alpha acids (bittering agents) going into the beer before fermentation. Equal to the weight of hops in ounces multiplied by the percentage of Alpha Acids.

Amylase An enzyme group that converts starches to sugars, consisting primarily of alpha and beta amylase. Also referred to as the diastatic enzymes.

Aroma hops Hops usually added in the last 5 minutes of the boil to impart a hop aroma. They do not contribute much bitterness.

Attenuation The degree of conversion of sugar to alcohol and carbon dioxide.

Base malt A malt such as pale malt that serves as the "backbone" of the beer, as well as the main sugar source for fermentation.

Beer Any beverage made by fermenting malted barley and seasoning with hops.

Bittering hops Hops used early in he boil to impart bitterness. They do not generally impart much flavor or aroma.

Bottle conditioning Carbonating beer with an additional fermentation in the bottle.

Brew-kettle The vessel in which the wort from the mash is boiled with hops. Also called a copper.

Brewer's yeast A yeast used or suitable for use in brewing; the dried pulverized cells of such a yeast (Saccharomyces cerevisiae) are used especially as a source of B-complex vitamins.

"Bright" beer Beer in which yeast is no longer in suspension.

Burton water Hard water from Burton-on-Trent, in England, which is a superior water for brewing. (You can use gypsum salts to create the same hardness.)

Carboy Large glass jar specifically designed to hold wort for fermenting and for aging beer. Carboys typically range in size from 13.6–27.25 liters (3–6 gallons/3½ –7¼ US gallons). They are superior to most types of plastic fermentation and aging vessels because they do not capture or transfer odors or flavors.

Copper Another name for the boiler. Copper finings, although they are not made from copper, are meant for use in the boiler.

Demijohn A glass fermentation vessel.

Diacetyl Fermentation by-product that may lend buttery or butterscotch notes to beer. This is considered an off-flavor in excessive amounts in any beer. Note that it is considered an off-flavor in most lagers in any amount. Can also be caused by contamination.

Diastatic The conversion of starches into sugars.

Dry hopping Adding hops to finished beer to provide hop aroma and flavor but no bitterness.

Esters Aromatic compounds formed from alcohols by yeast action. Typically, smell fruity.

Fermentation The conversion of wort to beer, a process by which yeast turns sugars into alcohol and carbon dioxide.

Fermenter The vessel in which fermentation takes place; typically, a glass carboy or food-grade plastic bucket for homebrewing applications.

Final gravity (FG) The finished beer gravity will range from 1.005–1.015, depending on the original gravity (OG) and type of yeast. The density of the wort after fermentation occurs.

Finings Use of Irish moss or isinglass (or other agents) to clarify beer.

Flavor hops Hops added to the boil within the last 20 minutes, imparting flavor and some aroma to the beer and the settling of the yeast out of solution.

Flocculation Used to measure the rate at which yeast settles to the bottom of the fermentation vessel.

Gelatin A colorless and tasteless protein used as a fining agent.

Grain bill A list of the types and quantities of malt and other grains used in a beer recipe.

Gravity Like density, gravity describes the concentration of malt sugar in the wort. The specific gravity of water is 1.000 at 15°C (59°F). Typical beer worts range from 1.035–1.055 before fermentation (OG). The finished beer gravity (FG) will range from 1.005–1.015, depending on the OG and type of yeast.

Grist The term for crushed malt before mashing.

Gypsous water See Burton water.

Gypsum salts Hydrated calcium sulphate used to treat soft or neutral water in order to make it hard.

Homebrew Used to describe an alcoholic drink, especially beer, brewed at home. Hence, homebrewer and homebrewing.

Hop strainer A device to help strain hops to improve clarification of beer.

Hydrometer Instrument that measures the density of liquid in comparison with the density of water. You can determine the alcohol percentage of a finished beer by comparing the original gravity and final gravity.

Insulated mash tun The double-jacketed, stainless-steel vessel in which mashing occurs.

International Bittering Units (IBU) A more precise unit for measuring hops. Equal to the AAU, multiplied by factors for percent utilization, wort volume and wort gravity.

Irish moss An emulsifying agent that promotes break-material formation and precipitation during the boil and upon cooling.

Isinglass The clear swim bladders of a species of small fish, consisting mainly of the structural protein collagen, which acts to absorb and precipitate yeast cells, via electrostatic binding.

Krausen Refers to the foamy head that builds on top of the beer during primary fermentation.

Lauter To strain or separate. Lautering separates the wort from the grain via filtering and sparging.

Lovibond Measurement against which malt and beer colors are compared. The higher the lovibond, the darker the color.

Malt Any grain (rye, wheat, barley, etc.) that has undergone the malting process.

Malt liquor A legal term used in the United States to designate a fermented beverage of relatively high alcohol content (7–8% by volume).

Mash Step-in, all-grain or partial mash brewing in which crushed grains/malt are mixed with hot water to rest at a pre-determined temperature.

Mash roll List of grain needed for a specific recipe.

Mash tun A tank where grist is soaked in water and heated in order to convert the starch to sugar and extract the sugars and other solubles from the grist.

Microbrewery Breweries and brewpubs producing less than 1,500 barrels per year.

Mini-pin A small barrel that holds 5 litres (1 gallon/1¼ US gallons) of liquid.

Original gravity The density of the wort before fermentation occurs.

Petillance Means slightly fizzy to tickle the tongue.

Pitch Term for adding the yeast to the fermenter.

Poly-pin A vessel that can hold 20.5 litres (4½ gallons/5 ½ US gallons).

Primary fermentation The high-activity phase marked by the evolution of carbon dioxide and krausen. Most of the attenuation occurs during this phase.

Priming The method of adding a small amount of fermentable sugar prior to bottling to give the beer carbonation.

Protofloc A type of copper fining available in tablet form. Add it toward the end of the boil to help remove protein from the wort, which could cause hazes in the finished beer.

Racking The careful siphoning of the beer away from the trub.

Runnings The liquid collected from the mash.

Secondary fermentation A period of settling and conditioning of the beer after primary fermentation and before bottling.

"Smack-pack" yeast A form of liquid yeast. Consists of a pouch of yeast with a smaller pouch of starter wort inside. Once "smacked," the inner pouch ruptures and the yeast will begin growing. The pouch will expand to about 5cm (2in) and will be ready to pitch within a couple of days.

Sodium ion A mineral that contributes to the perceived flavor of beer by enhancing its sweetness.

Sparge To sprinkle; to rinse the grain bed during lautering.

Strike water This is water that has been heated to the right temperature to add to the grist.

Tej A mead or honey wine that is brewed and consumed in Ethiopia. It is flavored with the powdered leaves and twigs of gesho (Rhamnus prinoides), a hop-like bittering agent that is a species of buckthorn.

Trub The sediment at the bottom of the fermenter, consisting of hops, hot and cold break material, and dormant (sometimes dead) yeast.

Wort The malt-sugar solution that is boiled with hops prior to fermentation.

Zymurgy The science of brewing and fermentation.

Useful Abbreviations

AA	apparent attenuation
ABV	alcohol by volume
ASBC	American Society of Brewing Chemists
CO_2	carbon dioxide
CRS	Carbonate Reducing Solution
DLS	Dry Liquor Salts
DME	Dry Malt Extract
EBC	European Brewery Convention
FG	Final Gravity
IBU	International Bittering Units
°L	Lovibond
OG	Original Gravity
SRM	Standard Reference Method

"Alcohol is necessary for a man so that he can have a good opinion of himself, undisturbed by the facts."

ANONYMOUS

EQUIPMENT SUPPLIERS

American Home Brew Supply
9295 Chesapeake Dr, Ste E
San Diego
California 92123
(858) 268-3024
www.redkart.com/ahbs

Beer Necessities
9850 Nesbit Ferry Road
Alpharetta
Georgia 30022
(770) 645-1777
www.beernecessities.com

Brew Brothers
2020 NW Aloclek Drive
Suite 104
Hillsboro
Oregon 97124
(971) 222 3434
www.brewbrothers.biz

Brooklyn Homebrew
163 8th Street
Brooklyn
New York 11215
(718) 369 0776
www.brooklyn-homebrew.com

Canadian Homebrew Supplies
10 Wilkinson Rd, Unit 1
Brampton
Ontario L6T 5B1
(905) 450-0191
www.homebrew-supplies.ca

Homebrew Headquarters
300 N. Colt Road, Suite 134
Richardson
Texas 75080
(972) 234-4411
www.homebrewhq.com

Home Sweet Homebrew
2008 Sansom Street
Philadelphia
PA 19103
(215) 569 9469
www.homesweethomebrew.com

Keystone Homebrew Supply
435 Doylestown Road (Rt. 202)
Montgomeryville
PA 18936
(215) 855-0100
www.keystonehomebrew.com

Listermann's Brewing Supplies
1621 Dana Avenue
Cincinnati
Ohio 45207
(513) 731-1130
www.listermann.com

Midwest Homebrewing and Winemaking Supplies
5825 Excelsior Blvd.
Minneapolis
MN 55416
(952) 925-9854
www.midwestsupplies.com

Northern Brewer Homebrew Supply
1150 Grand Avenue
St. Paul
Minnesota 55105
651-223-6114
www.northernbrewer.com

Riverside Wine and Spirits
600 Manufacturers Rd
Chattanooga
Tennessee 37405-3702
(423) 267-4305
www.riversidewine.com

Rocky Mountain Homebrew Supply
218 N 4000 E
Rigby
Idaho 83442
(208) 745 0866
www.rockymountainhomebrew.com

Southern Brewing & Winemaking
1717 East Busch Blvd.
Unit 805
Tampa
Florida 33612
(813) 374-2174
www.southernbrewingwinemaking.com

UK

Brew
Unit 11
Portway Business Centre
Salisbury
SP4 6QX
0844 7362672
www.brewuk.co.uk

The Brew Shop
48 Buxton Road
Heaviley
Stockport
SK2 6NB
0161 480 4880
www.thebrewshop.com

The Brewer's Tap
70 St James Way
Sidcup
Kent
DA14 5HF
0208 302 8202
www.brewerstap.co.uk

Brewstore
14 Elgin Terrace
Edinburgh
EH7 5NW
0131 466 6244
www.brewstore.co.uk

Burghley Homebrew
Calamity Gulch
Bridge Hill Road
Newborough
Cambridgeshire
PE6 7SA
01733 810259
www.burghley-homebrew.com

Easy Home Brew
Unit 19
Connect 10
Foster Road
Sevington
Ashford
Kent
TN24 0FE
01233 502269
www.easyhomebrew.co.uk

The Home Brew Centre
250 Freeman Street
Grimsby
DN32 9DR
01472 343435
www.homebrewcentregy.com

The Homebrew Shop
Unit 2
Blackwater Trading Estate
Blackwater Way
Aldershot
Hants
GU12 4DJ
01252 338045
www.the-home-brew-shop.co.uk

The Hop Shop
22 Dale Road
Mutley
Plymouth
Devon
PL4 6PE
01752 660382
www.hopshopuk.com

Love Brewing
591 West Derby Road
Liverpool
L13 8AE
www.lovebrewing.co.uk

The Online Homebrew Company
Unit 5 Parkside
Potters Way
Southend-on-Sea
Essex
SS2 5SJ
http://www.the-online-homebrew-company.co.uk

Things to Brew
Unit 2
Kershaws Garden Centre
Halifax Road
Brighouse
West Yorkshire
HD6 2QD
01484 401423
www.thingstobrew.co.uk

INDEX

ACKNOWLEDGMENTS

Both Dave and I would like to extend our thanks to our friends and families for being so supportive throughout the writing of this book, when we were holed up with nothing but beer and brewing on the agenda. We are especially thankful for the patient encouragement we received from our respective partners, Elli and Chris, and also from our children, who at times must have wondered if we would ever return from the world of brewing. So Florence, Charlie, Isabel, Oscar, Silas, Rose, and Arturo, thanks for being wonderful kids!

Thank you, too, to Pete Jorgensen for his patience throughout the project, Caroline West for her keen eye for detail, and Ashley Western for the great design.

We would also like to thank Gavin Kingcome and Luis Peral-Aranda for their hard work in making the whole book look fantastic.

And last but not least, another big thank you to my husband, Chris, who is always there.

Please visit www.beshlie.co.uk to read my latest blog entries.

Beshlie Grimes

Chart on p29 from Wikipedia, "Beer Measurement" http://en.wikipedia/wiki/Beer_measurement (as of November 6th, 2011, 19:11 GMT).